CALEB ROSS

Full Stack Development With ASP.NET core and Angular

Contents

Introduction: Navigating the Full Stack Landscape

Overview of Full Stack Development

In the rapidly evolving world of software development, the term "full stack" has become a buzzword for developers who have the capability to work across both the *frontend* and *backend* of an application. Full stack development refers to the combined expertise needed to handle the user-facing side of applications (frontend) and the server-side logic, database management, and APIs (backend). By bridging these two areas, full stack developers offer a comprehensive skill set that makes them valuable assets in the tech industry.

Historically, software development was divided into two main domains: *frontend development*, where the user interface (UI) and user experience (UX) are crafted, and *backend development*, which focuses on databases, servers, and APIs. Frontend development involved technologies like HTML, CSS, and JavaScript, while backend development leveraged languages like PHP, Java, Ruby, Python, or ASP.NET for server-side logic.

However, in recent years, the demand for developers who understand both areas—capable of building entire web applications independently—has skyrocketed. Full stack developers bring a unified perspective to development. This means they understand how backend processes can impact the frontend and vice versa, optimizing code and reducing bottlenecks during the development lifecycle.

Why Full Stack Development Matters

In today's tech landscape, companies seek faster development cycles with fewer silos between frontend and backend teams. A full stack developer can reduce this friction, leading to:

1. **Faster product iterations** – As full stack developers understand both aspects, they can swiftly pivot between UI modifications and backend adjustments without having to rely on another team.
2. **More efficient debugging** – Instead of separating the problem-solving process into frontend and backend concerns, a full stack developer can diagnose and resolve issues holistically, considering all parts of the stack.
3. **Greater flexibility** – In startups or agile teams where resources are tight, having a developer who can transition from building APIs to tweaking UI elements allows for greater adaptability.
4. **Optimized teamwork** – Full stack developers can effectively communicate with designers, frontend developers, and backend engineers, acting as a bridge between these specializations, ensuring projects run smoothly.

In essence, full stack development empowers developers to become versatile contributors in the software development lifecycle, which is why it has become an attractive path for many. Mastering full stack development not only enhances your value to employers but also enables you to tackle more challenging and rewarding projects independently.

Why ASP.NET Core and Angular?

When choosing technologies for full stack development, it's important to pick tools that provide robustness, scalability, and efficiency. ASP.NET Core and Angular are two of the most powerful and widely used frameworks for backend and frontend development, respectively. Together, they offer a potent combination for building modern, scalable, and high-performance web applications. Let's explore why they are a winning combination for full stack development.

ASP.NET Core: A Robust Backend Framework

ASP.NET Core, developed by Microsoft, is an open-source, cross-platform framework that allows developers to build web applications and services. It stands out because of its:

1. **Cross-platform support** – ASP.NET Core works on Windows, Linux, and macOS, which makes it flexible for various environments. This flexibility appeals to modern development teams that deploy applications on different platforms.
2. **Performance and scalability** – ASP.NET Core is built with performance in mind, making it one of the fastest frameworks available. This makes it an excellent choice for handling large-scale applications and high-traffic websites.
3. **Modular architecture** – ASP.NET Core uses a modular approach that lets you include only the components you need, resulting in more lightweight and efficient applications.
4. **Integration with modern DevOps** – ASP.NET Core seamlessly integrates with DevOps pipelines, enabling automated testing, continuous integration (CI), and continuous deployment (CD) workflows.
5. **Security** – ASP.NET Core provides built-in security features like authentication, authorization, and data protection, which are crucial for developing secure web applications.

One of the standout features of ASP.NET Core is its focus on RESTful APIs. RESTful APIs are essential for modern web applications as they enable the backend to communicate with various frontend technologies like Angular, React, or even mobile apps.

Angular: A Frontend Powerhouse

Angular, developed by Google, is a powerful TypeScript-based frontend framework. It has become one of the most popular frameworks for building dynamic and interactive web applications. Angular is widely recognized for its:

1. **Two-way data binding** – Angular's two-way data binding ensures that any changes to the UI instantly reflect in the model and vice versa. This makes real-time applications easier to build and maintain.
2. **Component-based architecture** – Angular follows a component-based approach, where the UI is broken down into reusable, modular pieces, making large applications more manageable.
3. **Typescript** – Angular is built with TypeScript, a superset of JavaScript that adds static typing to the language, making your code more predictable and less error-prone.
4. **Comprehensive tooling** – Angular's CLI (Command Line Interface) makes it easy to scaffold new projects, generate components, services, and modules, and streamline the development process.
5. **Reactive Programming with RxJS** – Angular's integration with RxJS (Reactive Extensions for JavaScript) allows developers to build highly responsive and event-driven applications, perfect for real-time applications like chat apps or live updates.

Why Combine ASP.NET Core and Angular?

ASP.NET Core and Angular complement each other perfectly in full stack development. ASP.NET Core offers a robust and scalable backend framework, while Angular provides a dynamic and powerful frontend framework. Together, they allow developers to build applications that are not only feature-rich but also performant and secure.

Here's why their combination is so effective:

1. **Separation of Concerns** – ASP.NET Core handles the backend logic, including data storage, authentication, and server-side processing, while Angular focuses on delivering a responsive and interactive user experience. This clear division of responsibility simplifies both development and maintenance.

2. **Single-page Applications (SPAs)** – Angular is ideal for building SPAs, where only the dynamic content is loaded without refreshing the entire page. ASP.NET Core's Web API seamlessly communicates with Angular, making the backend/frontend integration smooth.

3. **Cross-platform Compatibility** – With ASP.NET Core being cross-platform and Angular's compatibility with modern browsers, the combination allows for building applications that run on any platform or device.

4. **Enterprise-Grade Applications** – Many enterprise applications require both a powerful backend and a highly interactive frontend. This combination of ASP.NET Core and Angular is widely used in industries like finance, healthcare, and retail due to their robustness and ability to scale.

In short, ASP.NET Core and Angular provide the tools necessary to build modern, scalable, and high-performance full stack applications, making them a go-to choice for developers looking to deliver top-notch web solutions.

How This Book is Structured

To ensure a smooth learning experience, this book is structured in a logical progression, guiding you from foundational knowledge to advanced full stack development techniques. Whether you are new to ASP.NET Core and Angular or have some experience and want to master both frameworks, this book will serve as a comprehensive guide.

Part 1: Building Foundations

In the first part of the book, we will cover the essentials of both ASP.NET Core and Angular. This section will guide you through setting up your development environment, understanding the basics of each framework, and building a simple full stack application. Key chapters include:

- **Chapter 1**: Setting up ASP.NET Core and Angular
- **Chapter 2**: Backend Essentials with ASP.NET Core
- **Chapter 3**: Frontend Basics with Angular

Part 2: Intermediate Full Stack Development

After mastering the basics, Part 2 dives deeper into more complex topics like authentication, authorization, and integrating frontend and backend. You will learn how to implement user authentication, manage databases, and handle HTTP requests efficiently. Key chapters include:

- **Chapter 4**: Building APIs with ASP.NET Core
- **Chapter 5**: Making HTTP Requests in Angular
- **Chapter 6**: Implementing Authentication and Authorization

Part 3: Advanced Topics

In the final section of the book, we cover advanced topics that take your skills to the next level. You will learn how to optimize performance, secure your applications, and deploy them to the cloud. Key chapters include:

- **Chapter 7**: Real-Time Functionality with SignalR
- **Chapter 8**: Performance Optimization
- **Chapter 9**: Deploying to Azure and AWS

Hands-On Projects and Code Examples

Each chapter includes hands-on projects and code examples that reinforce your learning. By the end of each chapter, you will have built real-world applications that reflect industry practices. Additionally, you will have access to a GitHub repository containing all the code samples and project files for your reference.

Prerequisites and Tools You'll Need

Before diving into full stack development with ASP.NET Core and Angular, you should have a basic understanding of:

- **HTML, CSS, and JavaScript**: Familiarity with these core web technologies is essential for working on the frontend.
- **Object-Oriented Programming (OOP)**: A basic grasp of OOP concepts is useful for understanding both ASP.NET Core (C#) and Angular (TypeScript).
- **Databases and SQL**: Knowing how to interact with databases using SQL will help you grasp the backend concepts more quickly.

Development Tools

Here are the essential tools you'll need to follow along with the book:

1. **Visual Studio Code** – A lightweight, powerful code editor suitable for both frontend and backend development.
2. **Node.js and npm** – Node.js is a JavaScript runtime that allows you to run Angular on your local machine, and npm (Node Package Manager) is used to manage dependencies.
3. **.NET SDK** – The .NET SDK provides all the tools you need to develop ASP.NET Core applications.
4. **SQL Server** or **SQLite** – You'll need a relational database to store data, and SQL Server or SQLite is a good option for beginners.
5. **Postman** – A tool for testing APIs, which will be helpful when building and testing your ASP.NET Core backend.

With these tools and the foundational knowledge you'll gain from the early chapters, you'll be ready to embark on your full stack development journey.

Chapter 1: Getting Started with ASP.NET Core and Angular

Setting Up the Development Environment

T he first step toward becoming a proficient full stack developer is to ensure that your development environment is properly configured. Both ASP.NET Core and Angular have specific tools and dependencies that must be installed on your machine to get started. In this section, we will go over the setup process for both the backend (ASP.NET Core) and the frontend (Angular), as well as a few essential tools that will streamline your development process.

1.1.1 Setting Up ASP.NET Core

ASP.NET Core is a cross-platform framework that allows you to build high-performance web applications. It's important to ensure that your environment is equipped to handle development for ASP.NET Core, regardless of whether you're working on Windows, macOS, or Linux.

1.1.1.1 Installing .NET SDK

The first step in setting up ASP.NET Core is to install the .NET SDK (Software Development Kit). The SDK includes everything you need to build and run .NET applications, including ASP.NET Core web apps.

1. **Visit the .NET website:**
2. Go to the official .NET website to download the latest version of the .NET SDK.
3. **Choose the appropriate version:**
4. Download the SDK that matches your operating system. It's generally best to download the Long Term Support (LTS) version, which ensures stability and longevity for your projects.
5. **Install the SDK:**
6. Follow the installation instructions for your operating system:

- **Windows**: Download the installer and run it.
- **macOS**: Use the installer or, alternatively, install via Homebrew with brew install —cask dotnet-sdk.
- **Linux**: Follow the detailed instructions provided for your specific Linux distribution.

1. **Verify the installation:**
2. Once the installation is complete, verify it by opening your terminal or command prompt and typing:

```bash
Copy code
dotnet --version
```

1. This should return the version number of the SDK you installed, confirming a successful installation.

1.1.1.2 Installing Visual Studio Code

While there are several Integrated Development Environments (IDEs) available for .NET development, Visual Studio Code (VS Code) is a lightweight and versatile code editor that's widely used by developers across different stacks. It has excellent support for ASP.NET Core and Angular, and numerous extensions can enhance your productivity.

1. **Download Visual Studio Code:**
2. Visit the official VS Code website and download the version compatible with your operating system.
3. **Install Visual Studio Code:**
4. Run the installation file and follow the prompts to install the editor.
5. **Install Essential Extensions for ASP.NET Core:**
6. After installing VS Code, you'll want to add some extensions to make development smoother:

- **C# extension**: This extension provides C# IntelliSense, debugging, and other features for working with ASP.NET Core projects.
- **REST Client**: This extension allows you to test APIs directly within VS Code.
- **Prettier**: This is a code formatter that can help maintain consistent code style.

You can install these extensions by navigating to the Extensions panel on the left-hand sidebar of VS Code and searching for them by name.

1.1.1.3 SQL Server or SQLite for Database Development

For full stack development, you'll also need a database management system. ASP.NET Core applications typically use SQL databases, and there are several options available, including Microsoft SQL Server and SQLite.

1. **SQL Server**:
2. SQL Server is an enterprise-grade relational database management system (RDBMS) developed by Microsoft. You can download the Express edition for free, which is sufficient for development purposes.
3. **SQLite**:

4. For lightweight applications or testing, you might prefer using SQLite, a file-based database system. It doesn't require installation on your machine, making it easier to set up for small projects. You can use the built-in SQLite libraries that come with ASP.NET Core, and Visual Studio Code has extensions for managing SQLite databases directly from the editor.

1.1.2 Setting Up Angular

Angular is a powerful front-end framework developed by Google, and like ASP.NET Core, it has its own set of tools and dependencies that need to be installed.

1.1.2.1 Installing Node.js and npm

Node.js is a JavaScript runtime that allows Angular applications to run on your local machine. npm (Node Package Manager) is included with Node.js and is used to install Angular and other frontend libraries.

1. **Download Node.js:**
2. Go to the Node.js website and download the latest stable version (LTS version is recommended).
3. **Install Node.js:**
4. Run the installer and follow the prompts to complete the installation process. Node.js includes npm, so you don't need to install npm separately.
5. **Verify the installation:**
6. Once the installation is complete, verify it by running the following commands in your terminal:

```bash
Copy code
node --version
npm --version
```

1. This should return the version numbers of Node.js and npm.

1.1.2.2 Installing Angular CLI

The Angular CLI (Command Line Interface) is a powerful tool that helps streamline Angular development by providing commands for creating components, services, routing, and more.

1. **Install Angular CLI via npm:**
2. Run the following command in your terminal to install Angular CLI globally on your machine:

```bash
Copy code
npm install -g @angular/cli
```

1. **Verify the installation:**
2. After installation, verify it by running:

```bash
Copy code
ng --version
```

1. This should display the installed version of the Angular CLI.

1.1.2.3 Installing Visual Studio Code Extensions for Angular

VS Code is also an excellent choice for Angular development, with various extensions available to enhance your workflow:

- **Angular Snippets**: Provides TypeScript and HTML snippets for Angular development.

- **Angular Language Service**: Offers IntelliSense and code navigation for Angular templates.

Installing these extensions follows the same process as installing the C# extension.

Introduction to ASP.NET Core and Angular Frameworks

Before diving into project development, it's essential to have a basic understanding of what ASP.NET Core and Angular are, how they work, and why they're popular choices for full stack development.

1.2.1 What is ASP.NET Core?

ASP.NET Core is a high-performance, cross-platform web framework for building modern, cloud-based web applications. It's part of the larger .NET ecosystem, which includes a wide array of libraries, tools, and frameworks for building various types of applications.

1.2.1.1 Key Features of ASP.NET Core

ASP.NET Core offers several features that make it a popular choice for backend development:

- **Cross-platform**: ASP.NET Core can run on Windows, macOS, and Linux, making it highly versatile.
- **High Performance**: It's one of the fastest frameworks available for building web APIs.
- **Modular Architecture**: Developers can choose only the components they need, which results in leaner applications.
- **Unified MVC and Web API Frameworks**: ASP.NET Core merges the concepts of MVC (Model-View-Controller) and Web APIs, making it easier to build APIs alongside web applications.
- **Built-in Dependency Injection**: ASP.NET Core has dependency

injection as a first-class citizen, which helps keep your code modular and testable.

1.2.2 What is Angular?

Angular is a TypeScript-based front-end framework for building dynamic, single-page applications (SPAs). Developed by Google, it provides a robust platform for building complex, client-side applications that are fast, scalable, and maintainable.

1.2.2.1 Key Features of Angular

Some of Angular's standout features include:

- **Component-based Architecture**: Angular applications are built as a collection of reusable components, making large applications easier to manage and scale.
- **Two-way Data Binding**: Angular's two-way data binding automatically synchronizes the UI with the underlying data model, ensuring that any changes in one are instantly reflected in the other.
- **TypeScript Support**: Angular is built with TypeScript, which enhances JavaScript with static typing, making it easier to catch errors during development.
- **CLI (Command Line Interface)**: The Angular CLI simplifies the development process by providing built-in commands for generating components, services, modules, and more.
- **Reactive Programming**: Angular's integration with RxJS allows for efficient handling of asynchronous data streams, enabling the development of real-time, reactive applications.

Project Setup: Creating a Full Stack Application

Now that your development environment is ready and you have a basic understanding of ASP.NET Core and Angular, it's time to set up your first full stack application. In this section, we'll walk through creating a basic

ASP.NET Core backend and an Angular frontend, then connecting the two.

1.3.1 Creating an ASP.NET Core Project

To create an ASP.NET Core application, we'll use the .NET CLI, which is a command-line interface for building .NET applications.

1. **Open your terminal or command prompt** and navigate to the folder where you want to create your project.
2. **Create a new ASP.NET Core Web API project** by running the following command:

```bash
Copy code
dotnet new webapi -n FullStackApp
```

1. This will create a new Web API project named FullStackApp with the necessary files and folders.
2. **Navigate into the project folder**:

```bash
Copy code
cd FullStackApp
```

1. **Run the application** to make sure everything is set up correctly:

```bash
Copy code
dotnet run
```

1. This command will start the development server, and you should see output indicating that the application is running at http://localhost:500 0.

1.3.2 Creating an Angular Project

Next, we'll create the Angular frontend using the Angular CLI.

1. **Open a new terminal** window and navigate to the folder where you want to create your Angular project.
2. **Run the following command** to create a new Angular application:

```bash
Copy code
ng new FullStackAppClient
```

1. The Angular CLI will prompt you to choose a few options:

- Choose **Yes** when asked if you want to add Angular routing.
- Choose **SCSS** as the stylesheet format.

1. **Navigate into the project folder:**

```bash
Copy code
cd FullStackAppClient
```

1. **Run the Angular application** to ensure everything is set up correctly:

```bash
Copy code
ng serve
```

1. This will start the Angular development server, and you can view the application in your browser by visiting http://localhost:4200.

Running Your First Application

Now that both the ASP.NET Core backend and Angular frontend are set up, it's time to connect them and run the full stack application.

1.4.1 Configuring the Backend to Serve the Angular App

In many full stack applications, the backend serves both the API and the frontend static files. To achieve this, we need to configure ASP.NET Core to serve the Angular files after building the Angular project.

1. **Install the Angular build output to ASP.NET Core**:
2. First, build your Angular project for production by running:

```bash
Copy code
ng build --prod
```

1. This will create a dist/ folder with the compiled Angular app. Copy the contents of this folder into a new folder in your ASP.NET Core project, typically named ClientApp.
2. **Configure ASP.NET Core to Serve Static Files**:
3. Open Startup.cs in your ASP.NET Core project and configure the UseStaticFiles() middleware to serve the Angular files:

```csharp
Copy code
app.UseStaticFiles();
app.UseRouting();
app.UseEndpoints(endpoints =>
{
    endpoints.MapControllers();
    endpoints.MapFallbackToFile("index.html");
});
```

1. **Run Both Applications**:
2. Run both the ASP.NET Core and Angular applications. The backend will serve both the API and the Angular frontend, creating a unified full stack application.
3. **Test the Application**:
4. Open your browser and navigate to http://localhost:5000. You should see your Angular app running, and any API calls made by the Angular frontend will be routed through the ASP.NET Core backend.

Conclusion

By the end of this chapter, you've successfully set up the development environment, created both an ASP.NET Core backend and an Angular frontend, and run your first full stack application. The project is simple for now, but in the upcoming chapters, we'll expand on this foundation, adding more features, handling data, and exploring the powerful tools both ASP.NET Core and Angular offer.

This first step is crucial for understanding the basics, and now that everything is set up, we're ready to dive deeper into the exciting world of full stack development.

Chapter 2: Understanding the ASP.NET Core Backend

ASP.NET Core Project Structure

When working with ASP.NET Core, it's crucial to understand the project structure and how each part contributes to the overall functionality of your web application. In this section, we will explore the basic files and folders that come with a new ASP.NET Core project, what they do, and how you can interact with them.

2.1.1 Files and Folders in an ASP.NET Core Project

When you create a new ASP.NET Core project using the dotnet new command, the framework automatically generates a set of files and folders that form the skeleton of your application. These files include everything you need to build, run, and deploy your ASP.NET Core app. Let's break down the key components:

2.1.1.1 The Program.cs File

The Program.cs file is the entry point for your application. It contains the Main() method, which is where the application starts. The Main() method in ASP.NET Core uses a Host object to configure and run the web application.

Here's an example of what the Program.cs file looks like:

```csharp
Copy code
public class Program
{
    public static void Main(string[] args)
    {
        CreateHostBuilder(args).Build().Run();
    }

    public static IHostBuilder CreateHostBuilder(string[] args) =>
        Host.CreateDefaultBuilder(args)
            .ConfigureWebHostDefaults(webBuilder =>
            {
                webBuilder.UseStartup<Startup>();
            });
}
```

This file contains the core logic for creating and configuring the web server. In most cases, you won't need to modify this file frequently. However, understanding its role is crucial for knowing how ASP.NET Core applications are initiated.

2.1.1.2 The Startup.cs File

The Startup.cs file is one of the most important files in an ASP.NET Core project. It defines how the application will respond to incoming requests. This file contains two key methods:

1. **ConfigureServices** – This method is where you register services that your app will use, such as dependency injection, authentication, and database connections.
2. **Configure** – This method sets up the request pipeline for your application. Middleware components are added here, which handle everything from routing to error handling.

Here's a basic example of a Startup.cs file:

```csharp
Copy code
public class Startup
{
    public Startup(IConfiguration configuration)
    {
        Configuration = configuration;
    }

    public IConfiguration Configuration { get; }

    public void ConfigureServices(IServiceCollection services)
    {
        services.AddControllers();
    }

    public void Configure(IApplicationBuilder app,
    IWebHostEnvironment env)
    {
        if (env.IsDevelopment())
        {
            app.UseDeveloperExceptionPage();
        }
        else
        {
            app.UseExceptionHandler("/Home/Error");
            app.UseHsts();
        }

        app.UseHttpsRedirection();
        app.UseStaticFiles();
        app.UseRouting();
        app.UseAuthorization();

        app.UseEndpoints(endpoints =>
        {
            endpoints.MapControllers();
        });
```

```
    }
}
```

In this file, ConfigureServices registers services like controllers, while Configure defines the middleware that manages how the application handles HTTP requests.

2.1.1.3 The Controllers Folder

The Controllers folder is where you define your application's controllers, which handle incoming HTTP requests and return responses. Controllers are a key part of the MVC (Model-View-Controller) pattern, and we'll explore them in more detail later in this chapter.

For now, just know that the Controllers folder will contain the classes that define how your application responds to requests at specific endpoints.

2.1.1.4 The appsettings.json File

The appsettings.json file is used to store configuration settings for your application. This is where you define things like database connection strings, third-party service keys, and other settings that vary between development, staging, and production environments.

Here's an example of what an appsettings.json file might look like:

```json
Copy code
{
  "Logging": {
    "LogLevel": {
      "Default": "Information",
      "Microsoft": "Warning",
      "Microsoft.Hosting.Lifetime": "Information"
    }
  },
  "AllowedHosts": "*",
  "ConnectionStrings": {
    "DefaultConnection": "Server=
(localdb)\\mssqllocaldb;Database=
MyAppDB;Trusted_Connection=True;"
```

```
    }
  }
```

This file is crucial for managing configuration across different environments without hardcoding sensitive data into your application.

2.1.1.5 The wwwroot Folder

The wwwroot folder is the location where static files (CSS, JavaScript, images, etc.) are stored. ASP.NET Core serves files directly from this folder when users request them.

For example, if you have an image file located at wwwroot/images/logo.png, you can reference it in your application as /images/logo.png.

2.1.2 The MVC Pattern in ASP.NET Core

ASP.NET Core uses the MVC (Model-View-Controller) design pattern, which separates the concerns of your application into three components:

- **Model** – Represents the data and business logic of the application.
- **View** – Handles the presentation of the data (usually HTML for web applications).
- **Controller** – Manages the interaction between the Model and the View, handling user requests, processing them, and returning responses.

This separation of concerns makes it easier to manage and scale large applications. While ASP.NET Core is often associated with MVC for building traditional web applications, it's also a powerful platform for creating APIs, which will be our focus in this book.

Introduction to Controllers, Routing, and Middleware

Now that we have a good understanding of the basic project structure, it's time to dive deeper into some core ASP.NET Core concepts: controllers, routing, and middleware.

2.2.1 What are Controllers?

In ASP.NET Core, controllers are responsible for handling incoming HTTP requests, processing them, and returning appropriate responses. In web APIs, controllers often return data in the form of JSON, but they can also return HTML views in MVC applications.

Controllers are defined as classes, and each method within a controller is typically mapped to an HTTP verb (GET, POST, PUT, DELETE) to perform different actions.

Here's an example of a simple controller:

```csharp
Copy code
[ApiController]
[Route("api/[controller]")]
public class WeatherController : ControllerBase
{
    [HttpGet]
    public IActionResult GetWeather()
    {
        var weatherData = new { Temperature = 72, Condition =
        "Sunny" };
        return Ok(weatherData);
    }
}
```

In this example:

- The ApiController attribute indicates that this controller is designed to serve APIs.
- The Route attribute defines the URL pattern that this controller will respond to. In this case, it will respond to api/weather.
- The HttpGet attribute specifies that the GetWeather method will handle GET requests.
- The Ok() method is used to return a 200 OK status code along with the weatherData as a JSON response.

2.2.1.1 Actions in Controllers

An action is any public method in a controller class that handles incoming requests. Each action corresponds to a specific route and HTTP method (GET, POST, etc.). For example:

```csharp
Copy code
[HttpPost]
public IActionResult PostWeather([FromBody] WeatherRequest
weatherRequest)
{
    // Process the weather request and return a response.
    return CreatedAtAction(nameof(GetWeather), new { id = 1 },
    weatherRequest);
}
```

In this example, the PostWeather method handles POST requests, and it accepts a parameter from the request body using the [FromBody] attribute.

2.2.2 Routing in ASP.NET Core

Routing in ASP.NET Core is the mechanism that maps incoming HTTP requests to the appropriate controllers and actions. Routes are defined in two main ways:

- **Attribute-based routing** – Routes are defined using attributes in the controller classes.
- **Convention-based routing** – Routes are defined globally in the Startup.cs file.

2.2.2.1 Attribute-based Routing

In attribute-based routing, you define routes directly in your controller classes using the [Route] attribute.

For example:

```csharp
Copy code
[ApiController]
[Route("api/weather")]
public class WeatherController : ControllerBase
{
    [HttpGet]
    public IActionResult GetWeather()
    {
        // Action for GET requests to /api/weather
        return Ok();
    }

    [HttpGet("{id}")]
    public IActionResult GetWeatherById(int id)
    {
        // Action for GET requests to /api/weather/{id}
        return Ok(id);
    }
}
```

In this example, two routes are defined:

- api/weather – This route maps to the GetWeather method.
- api/weather/{id} – This route maps to the GetWeatherById method, where {id} is a parameter.

Chapter 3: Diving into Angular Frontend Development

Angular is one of the most popular frameworks for building dynamic, responsive, and scalable web applications. It's known for its component-based architecture, two-way data binding, and powerful tools for creating single-page applications (SPAs). In this chapter, we will take a detailed look at Angular's project structure, components, modules, and templates, and explore key concepts like two-way data binding and directives. By the end of this chapter, you'll be well-equipped to build and run a basic Angular application.

Understanding Angular Project Structure

Before diving into coding, it's essential to understand how Angular organizes its files and directories. Angular projects follow a highly organized structure to promote scalability, maintainability, and readability. This structure is automatically created when you generate a new Angular project using the Angular CLI.

Let's start by examining the basic files and folders in an Angular project, understanding their purposes, and how they fit into the development workflow.

3.1.1 Files and Folders in an Angular Project

After creating a new Angular project with the Angular CLI (ng new command), you will see several files and folders in your project directory. Here's a breakdown of the key components:

3.1.1.1 The src/ Folder

The src/ folder is the core of your Angular project, containing all the files and resources needed to build your application. Inside the src/ folder, you'll find the following subfolders and files:

- **app/**: This is where most of your application's code resides, including components, services, and modules.
- **assets/**: Static assets like images, fonts, and JSON files are stored here.
- **environments/**: This folder contains environment-specific configuration files, such as environment variables for development or production.
- **index.html**: The main HTML file where Angular injects the app. This file serves as the entry point for the entire application.
- **main.ts**: The main TypeScript file that bootstraps the Angular application.
- **styles.css**: The global CSS file where you can define styles that apply to the entire application.
- **polyfills.ts**: This file includes polyfills to ensure compatibility with older browsers.

3.1.1.2 The app/ Folder

The app/ folder is where the heart of your Angular application lives. It contains the components, modules, and services that make up your application. Initially, when you create a new Angular project, you'll find some default files here, including:

- **app.module.ts**: The root module of your application. It declares the components and imports the necessary Angular modules.
- **app.component.ts**: The root component of your application. This

component is automatically created and serves as the main container for other components.

- **app.component.html**: The template for the root component, which defines the UI of the main component.
- **app.component.css**: The CSS file for styling the root component.

We'll explore each of these in detail as we build out our first Angular application.

Components, Modules, and Templates in Angular

Angular is built around the idea of reusability, modularity, and separation of concerns. The framework is primarily composed of three key building blocks: **components**, **modules**, and **templates**. Together, these form the core structure of Angular applications.

3.2.1 Components in Angular

Components are the fundamental building blocks of an Angular application. Each component controls a portion of the view (UI), and it consists of three main parts:

- **A template** (HTML): Defines the component's UI.
- **A class** (TypeScript): Contains the logic and data for the component.
- **A stylesheet** (CSS or SCSS): Defines the component's appearance.

3.2.1.1 Anatomy of a Component

Let's take a closer look at a basic Angular component, using the default AppComponent generated when you create a new Angular project:

app.component.ts:

```typescript
typescript
Copy code
import { Component } from '@angular/core';

@Component({
  selector: 'app-root',
  templateUrl: './app.component.html',
  styleUrls: ['./app.component.css']
})
export class AppComponent {
  title = 'Angular Basics';
}
```

- **@Component decorator**: This is a special TypeScript decorator that defines the component's metadata. It includes the following properties:
- **selector**: This defines the custom HTML tag (<app-root>) that will represent this component in the DOM.
- **templateUrl**: Specifies the HTML file for the component's template.
- **styleUrls**: Points to the CSS or SCSS files that contain the styles for this component.
- **Class**: The AppComponent class contains the logic for the component. In this case, it defines a title property that is displayed in the template.

3.2.1.2 The Component Lifecycle

Angular components go through a series of lifecycle events, from creation to destruction. Understanding these lifecycle hooks helps you manage component behavior and optimize performance.

The main lifecycle hooks include:

- **ngOnInit**: Called once the component is initialized.
- **ngOnChanges**: Triggered whenever the component's input properties change.
- **ngOnDestroy**: Called just before the component is destroyed.

For example, to add initialization logic to your component, you can use the ngOnInit hook:

```typescript
Copy code
export class AppComponent implements OnInit {
  title = 'Angular Basics';

  ngOnInit() {
    console.log('Component Initialized');
  }
}
```

3.2.2 Modules in Angular

Modules are containers for different parts of your Angular application, such as components, services, and other modules. Every Angular application must have at least one module, known as the root module, which is typically named AppModule.

3.2.2.1 Root Module: AppModule

The root module is defined in the app.module.ts file, and it serves as the entry point for the application. Here's an example of a basic AppModule:

```typescript
Copy code
import { NgModule } from '@angular/core';
import { BrowserModule } from '@angular/platform-browser';
import { AppComponent } from './app.component';

@NgModule({
  declarations: [
    AppComponent
  ],
  imports: [
    BrowserModule
  ],
```

```
  providers: [],
  bootstrap: [AppComponent]
})
export class AppModule { }
```

- **NgModule decorator**: This is used to define an Angular module and its metadata.
- **declarations**: Lists all the components, directives, and pipes that belong to this module.
- **imports**: Specifies other modules that this module depends on, such as BrowserModule, which is necessary for any web application.
- **bootstrap**: Defines the root component that Angular should bootstrap when the application starts.

As your application grows, you can create feature modules to encapsulate specific functionality, making your app more modular and maintainable.

3.2.3 Templates in Angular

Templates define the HTML that renders the component's view. Templates can contain regular HTML as well as Angular's own syntax for rendering dynamic content, handling events, and binding data.

3.2.3.1 Interpolation in Templates

Interpolation is used to bind a component's property to the template, allowing dynamic content to be displayed in the view. This is done using double curly braces ({{}}).

For example, in the app.component.html file:

```html
Copy code
<h1>{{ title }}</h1>
```

In this case, the title property from AppComponent is rendered within the <h1> tag.

3.2.3.2 Property Binding

Property binding is used to set the value of an element's attribute dynamically. This is done using square brackets ([]).

Example:

```html
Copy code
<img [src]="imageUrl" alt="Angular Logo">
```

In this example, the src attribute of the <img> element is bound to the imageUrl property in the component class.

3.2.3.3 Event Binding

Event binding allows you to respond to user actions such as clicks, key presses, or form submissions. This is done using parentheses (()).

Example:

```html
Copy code
<button (click)="onButtonClick()">Click me</button>
```

The click event is bound to the onButtonClick method in the component class, which is triggered when the button is clicked.

Two-Way Data Binding and Directives

One of Angular's most powerful features is two-way data binding, which allows synchronization between the model and the view. In addition, directives provide powerful ways to manipulate the DOM and extend HTML's functionality.

3.3.1 Two-Way Data Binding

Two-way data binding allows the view and the model to stay in sync: when the model changes, the view is updated automatically, and when the view changes (e.g., user input), the model is updated as well.

3.3.1.1 Using ngModel for Two-Way Data Binding

In Angular, two-way data binding is implemented using the ngModel directive, which is typically used with form elements.

For example:

```html
html
Copy code
<input [(ngModel)]="name" placeholder="Enter your name">
<p>Your name is: {{ name }}</p>
```

Here's what happens:

- The input field is bound to the name property in the component class using ngModel.
- When the user types into the input field, the name property is updated automatically, and the new value is displayed in the <p> element.

To use ngModel, you need to import the FormsModule into your AppModule:

```typescript
typescript
Copy code
import { NgModule } from '@angular/core';
import { BrowserModule } from '@angular/platform-browser';
import { FormsModule } from '@angular/forms';  // Import
FormsModule
import { AppComponent } from './app.component';

@NgModule({
  declarations: [AppComponent],
  imports: [BrowserModule, FormsModule],  // Add FormsModule to
```

```
  imports
  providers: [],
  bootstrap: [AppComponent]
})
export class AppModule {}
```

3.3.2 Directives in Angular

Directives are special markers in the DOM that tell Angular to do something with a DOM element or component. Angular provides several built-in directives, and you can also create custom directives to extend functionality.

3.3.2.1 Structural Directives

Structural directives change the structure of the DOM by adding or removing elements. The most common structural directives are *ngIf and *ngFor.

- ***ngIf**: Displays an element only if a condition is true.

Example:

```html
Copy code
<p *ngIf="isLoggedIn">Welcome, user!</p>
```

If isLoggedIn is true, the <p> element will be displayed. If it's false, the element is removed from the DOM.

- ***ngFor**: Iterates over a collection and renders a template for each item.

Example:

```html
Copy code
<ul>
  <li *ngFor="let item of items">{{ item }}</li>
</ul>
```

This directive loops through the items array and displays each item in a <li> element.

3.3.2.2 Attribute Directives

Attribute directives change the appearance or behavior of an element. One of the most common attribute directives is ngClass, which adds or removes CSS classes dynamically.

Example:

```html
Copy code
<div [ngClass]="{ 'active': isActive }">This div is active</div>
```

If isActive is true, the active class is added to the <div>. If false, the class is removed.

Building a Basic Angular Application

Now that we have covered the fundamental concepts of Angular's project structure, components, modules, templates, two-way data binding, and directives, let's put it all together by building a basic Angular application.

3.4.1 Creating the Application

We will build a simple task manager app where users can add and display tasks. This example will demonstrate how to use components, data binding, and directives in a real-world scenario.

Step 1: Generate the Project

Use the Angular CLI to create a new project:

```bash
Copy code
ng new task-manager
```

Navigate into the project directory:

```bash
Copy code
cd task-manager
```

Step 2: Create a Task Component

Generate a new component for managing tasks:

```bash
Copy code
ng generate component task
```

This command will create four files:

- task.component.ts
- task.component.html
- task.component.css
- task.component.spec.ts

Step 3: Update the Task Component

Let's modify the task.component.ts file to add logic for managing tasks:

```typescript
Copy code
import { Component } from '@angular/core';
```

```
@Component({
  selector: 'app-task',
  templateUrl: './task.component.html',
  styleUrls: ['./task.component.css']
})
export class TaskComponent {
  tasks: string[] = [];
  newTask: string = '';

  addTask() {
    if (this.newTask) {
      this.tasks.push(this.newTask);
      this.newTask = '';
    }
  }

  removeTask(index: number) {
    this.tasks.splice(index, 1);
  }
}
```

In this example:

- tasks is an array that stores the list of tasks.
- newTask is a string that stores the user input.
- addTask() adds a new task to the list.
- removeTask() removes a task from the list by index.

Step 4: Update the Task Component Template

Next, we'll update the task.component.html template to allow users to add and display tasks:

```html
Copy code
<h1>Task Manager</h1>

<input [(ngModel)]="newTask" placeholder="Enter a task">
```

```
<button (click)="addTask()">Add Task</button>

<ul>
  <li *ngFor="let task of tasks; let i = index">
    {{ task }}
    <button (click)="removeTask(i)">Remove</button>
  </li>
</ul>
```

- The input field is bound to newTask using two-way data binding (ngModel).
- The *ngFor directive is used to display the list of tasks.
- The addTask() and removeTask() methods are triggered by button clicks.

Step 5: Add FormsModule to the App Module

Since we're using ngModel for two-way data binding, we need to import FormsModule in the app.module.ts file:

```typescript
Copy code
import { NgModule } from '@angular/core';
import { BrowserModule } from '@angular/platform-browser';
import { FormsModule } from '@angular/forms';
import { AppComponent } from './app.component';
import { TaskComponent } from './task/task.component';

@NgModule({
  declarations: [
    AppComponent,
    TaskComponent
  ],
  imports: [
    BrowserModule,
    FormsModule
  ],
  providers: [],
```

```
    bootstrap: [AppComponent]
})
export class AppModule { }
```

Step 6: Run the Application

Finally, run the application using the Angular CLI:

```bash
Copy code
ng serve
```

Navigate to http://localhost:4200 in your browser, and you should see the task manager application running. You can now add and remove tasks using the interface.

Conclusion

In this chapter, you've learned about the core concepts of Angular, including its project structure, components, modules, templates, two-way data binding, and directives. You've also built a basic task manager application to put these concepts into practice. These building blocks form the foundation of Angular development, and as you progress through the book, you'll explore more advanced topics and build increasingly complex applications.

Chapter 4: Connecting the Dots: Integrating Frontend and Backend

I n modern web applications, the frontend and backend must work seamlessly together to provide a smooth user experience. This chapter will guide you through the process of integrating your Angular frontend with your ASP.NET Core backend. You'll learn about RESTful services, how to make API calls from Angular, configure Cross-Origin Resource Sharing (CORS), and display data fetched from your backend in your Angular application.

Understanding RESTful Services and HTTP

4.1.1 What are RESTful Services?

REST (Representational State Transfer) is an architectural style that defines a set of constraints for building web services. RESTful services are web services that adhere to these constraints, making them stateless, scalable, and easy to consume over HTTP.

4.1.1.1 Principles of REST

The core principles of RESTful architecture include:

1. **Statelessness**: Each request from the client to the server must contain

all the information needed to understand and process the request. The server does not store any client context between requests.

2. **Resource-based**: RESTful services expose resources (data entities) identified by URIs (Uniform Resource Identifiers). Resources can be represented in different formats, such as JSON or XML.

3. **HTTP Methods**: RESTful services leverage standard HTTP methods to perform actions on resources:

- **GET**: Retrieve data from the server.
- **POST**: Create a new resource on the server.
- **PUT**: Update an existing resource on the server.
- **DELETE**: Remove a resource from the server.

1. **Representation**: Resources can be represented in various formats, with JSON being the most commonly used format in web APIs due to its lightweight nature and compatibility with JavaScript.

2. **Stateless Communication**: Each interaction is independent, and the client should provide all necessary information to complete the request.

4.1.2 The Role of HTTP in RESTful Services

HTTP (Hypertext Transfer Protocol) is the foundation of data communication on the web. RESTful services utilize HTTP for communication between clients and servers. Each HTTP request and response contains important information, including the method, headers, and body.

4.1.2.1 HTTP Request Components

An HTTP request consists of the following components:

- **HTTP Method**: Specifies the action to be performed (GET, POST, PUT, DELETE).
- **URI**: The endpoint that identifies the resource being accessed.
- **Headers**: Metadata sent with the request, such as authentication tokens and content type.

- **Body**: Data sent with the request, typically used in POST and PUT requests.

Example of a simple HTTP GET request:

```vbnet
Copy code
GET /api/tasks HTTP/1.1
Host: localhost:5000
Accept: application/json
Authorization: Bearer <token>
```

4.1.2.2 HTTP Response Components

An HTTP response consists of:

- **Status Code**: Indicates the outcome of the request (e.g., 200 OK, 404 Not Found, 500 Internal Server Error).
- **Headers**: Metadata returned with the response.
- **Body**: The data returned by the server, often in JSON format.

Example of a simple HTTP response:

```css
Copy code
HTTP/1.1 200 OK
Content-Type: application/json

[
  { "id": 1, "task": "Learn Angular" },
  { "id": 2, "task": "Build an API" }
]
```

4.1.3 Designing RESTful APIs in ASP.NET Core

Now that we have a foundational understanding of RESTful services and HTTP, let's explore how to design RESTful APIs in ASP.NET Core. This section will guide you through creating a simple API for managing tasks, which will be consumed by your Angular application.

4.1.3.1 Creating the Task Model

Start by defining a Task model in the ASP.NET Core project. Create a new class called TaskModel.cs in the Models folder:

```csharp
Copy code
namespace FullStackApp.Models
{
    public class TaskModel
    {
        public int Id { get; set; }
        public string Task { get; set; }
        public bool IsCompleted { get; set; }
    }
}
```

4.1.3.2 Creating the Task Controller

Next, create a controller to handle the API requests. Create a new file called TasksController.cs in the Controllers folder:

```csharp
Copy code
using Microsoft.AspNetCore.Mvc;
using FullStackApp.Models;
using System.Collections.Generic;
using System.Linq;

namespace FullStackApp.Controllers
{
    [ApiController]
```

```csharp
[Route("api/[controller]")]
public class TasksController : ControllerBase
{
    private static List<TaskModel> tasks = new List<TaskModel>
    {
        new TaskModel { Id = 1, Task = "Learn Angular",
        IsCompleted = false },
        new TaskModel { Id = 2, Task = "Build an API",
        IsCompleted = false }
    };

    [HttpGet]
    public ActionResult<IEnumerable<TaskModel>> GetTasks()
    {
        return Ok(tasks);
    }

    [HttpPost]
    public ActionResult<TaskModel> AddTask(TaskModel task)
    {
        task.Id = tasks.Max(t => t.Id) + 1;
        tasks.Add(task);
        return CreatedAtAction(nameof(GetTasks), new { id =
        task.Id }, task);
    }

    [HttpDelete("{id}")]
    public IActionResult DeleteTask(int id)
    {
        var task = tasks.FirstOrDefault(t => t.Id == id);
        if (task == null)
        {
            return NotFound();
        }
        tasks.Remove(task);
        return NoContent();
    }
}
}
```

- **GetTasks()**: Returns a list of all tasks.
- **AddTask()**: Adds a new task to the list.
- **DeleteTask()**: Deletes a task by its ID.

Making API Calls from Angular

With our ASP.NET Core API set up, it's time to connect our Angular application to this API. We'll learn how to make HTTP requests from Angular to the ASP.NET Core backend to fetch and manipulate task data.

4.2.1 Setting Up the Angular HTTP Client

To make HTTP requests in Angular, we need to import the HttpClientModule in our application module. This module provides the necessary services to perform HTTP requests.

4.2.1.1 Importing HttpClientModule

Open the app.module.ts file and import the HttpClientModule:

```typescript
Copy code
import { HttpClientModule } from '@angular/common/http';

@NgModule({
  declarations: [
    AppComponent,
    TaskComponent
  ],
  imports: [
    BrowserModule,
    FormsModule,
    HttpClientModule  // Import HttpClientModule
  ],
  providers: [],
  bootstrap: [AppComponent]
})
export class AppModule { }
```

4.2.2 Creating a Task Service

It's a good practice to create a service in Angular to manage API calls. This keeps the component code clean and separates concerns. Let's create a Task service to interact with the backend API.

4.2.2.1 Generating the Task Service

Run the following command to generate a new service:

```bash
Copy code
ng generate service task
```

This will create two files: task.service.ts and task.service.spec.ts.

4.2.2.2 Implementing the Task Service

Open task.service.ts and implement methods for fetching, adding, and deleting tasks:

```typescript
Copy code
import { Injectable } from '@angular/core';
import { HttpClient } from '@angular/common/http';
import { Observable } from 'rxjs';
import { Task } from './task.model'; // Assuming you create a
model for Task

@Injectable({
  providedIn: 'root'
})
export class TaskService {
  private apiUrl = 'http://localhost:5000/api/tasks'; // URL of
  your ASP.NET Core API

  constructor(private http: HttpClient) { }

  getTasks(): Observable<Task[]> {
    return this.http.get<Task[]>(this.apiUrl);
```

```
  }

  addTask(task: Task): Observable<Task> {
    return this.http.post<Task>(this.apiUrl, task);
  }

  deleteTask(id: number): Observable<void> {
    return this.http.delete<void>(`${this.apiUrl}/${id}`);
  }
}
```

4.2.3 Using the Task Service in the Component

Now that we have our service set up, let's modify the TaskComponent to use this service to fetch and manipulate task data.

4.2.3.1 Injecting the Task Service

Open task.component.ts and inject the TaskService in the constructor:

```typescript
Copy code
import { Component, OnInit } from '@angular/core';
import { TaskService } from '../task.service';
import { Task } from './task.model';

@Component({
  selector: 'app-task',
  templateUrl: './task.component.html',
  styleUrls: ['./task.component.css']
})
export class TaskComponent implements OnInit {
  tasks: Task[] = [];
  newTask: string = '';

  constructor(private taskService: TaskService) { }

  ngOnInit() {
```

```
    this.loadTasks();
  }

  loadTasks() {
    this.taskService.getTasks().subscribe(tasks => {
      this.tasks = tasks;
    });
  }

  addTask() {
    if (this.newTask) {
      const task: Task = { task: this.newTask, isCompleted: false
      };
      this.taskService.addTask(task).subscribe(addedTask => {
        this.tasks.push(addedTask);
        this.newTask = '';
      });
    }
  }

  removeTask(id: number) {
    this.taskService.deleteTask(id).subscribe(() => {
      this.tasks = this.tasks.filter(t => t.id !== id);
    });
  }
}
```

In this example:

- The loadTasks() method fetches the task list from the API when the component initializes.
- The addTask() method sends a new task to the API and updates the local task list.
- The removeTask() method deletes a task by ID and updates the local task list accordingly.

4.2.4 *Updating the Task Component Template*

Let's update the task.component.html template to reflect the API integration:

```html
Copy code
<h1>Task Manager</h1>

<input [(ngModel)]="newTask" placeholder="Enter a task">
<button (click)="addTask()">Add Task</button>

<ul>
  <li *ngFor="let task of tasks; let i = index">
    {{ task.task }}
    <button (click)="removeTask(task.id)">Remove</button>
  </li>
</ul>
```

4.2.5 *Running the Application*

Make sure your ASP.NET Core backend is running, then start your Angular application:

```bash
Copy code
ng serve
```

Navigate to http://localhost:4200, and you should be able to add and remove tasks, which are managed via the ASP.NET Core API.

Cross-Origin Resource Sharing (CORS) Configuration

When developing applications that connect a frontend (Angular) to a backend (ASP.NET Core), you may encounter issues related to cross-origin requests. CORS is a security feature implemented by browsers to prevent malicious websites from making requests to a different domain than the one that served the web page. If your Angular application is running on a different port (or domain) than your ASP.NET Core API, you'll need to configure CORS to allow these requests.

4.3.1 What is CORS?

CORS (Cross-Origin Resource Sharing) is a mechanism that allows restricted resources on a web page to be requested from another domain outside the domain from which the resource originated. It defines a way for browsers to allow or deny requests based on the origin of the request.

4.3.2 Configuring CORS in ASP.NET Core

To enable CORS in your ASP.NET Core application, you need to update the Startup.cs file. Here's how you can do it:

4.3.2.1 Adding CORS Services

In the ConfigureServices method of your Startup.cs file, add CORS services and define the allowed origins:

```csharp
Copy code
public void ConfigureServices(IServiceCollection services)
{
    services.AddControllers();
    services.AddCors(options =>
    {
        options.AddPolicy("AllowAllOrigins",
            builder => builder.AllowAnyOrigin()
                            .AllowAnyMethod()
                            .AllowAnyHeader());
    });
}
```

In this configuration:

- The AllowAllOrigins policy permits requests from any origin, allows any HTTP method, and accepts any headers. This is useful for development but may need to be restricted in a production environment.

4.3.2.2 Applying the CORS Policy

Next, apply the CORS policy in the Configure method:

```csharp
Copy code
public void Configure(IApplicationBuilder app, IWebHostEnvironment env)
{
    if (env.IsDevelopment())
    {
        app.UseDeveloperExceptionPage();
    }
    else
    {
        app.UseExceptionHandler("/Home/Error");
        app.UseHsts();
    }

    app.UseHttpsRedirection();
    app.UseStaticFiles();

    // Apply CORS policy
    app.UseRouting();
    app.UseCors("AllowAllOrigins");   // Enable CORS

    app.UseAuthorization();

    app.UseEndpoints(endpoints =>
    {
        endpoints.MapControllers();
    });
}
```

4.3.3 Testing CORS Configuration

With CORS configured, you can test your Angular application by trying to make requests to the ASP.NET Core API. Open your Angular application in a browser, and try adding and removing tasks. If configured correctly, you should not encounter any CORS-related errors.

Displaying Data from the ASP.NET Core Backend in Angular

With the integration of the backend API and the Angular frontend complete, the final step is to ensure that the data fetched from the ASP.NET Core backend is displayed correctly in your Angular application.

4.4.1 Data Binding in Angular

Angular makes it easy to display data from the backend by leveraging its data-binding capabilities. When you fetch data from the API and store it in a component property, Angular's binding system ensures that the UI updates automatically whenever that property changes.

4.4.2 Using Observables with HTTP Requests

When making HTTP requests in Angular, you typically work with Observables, which are part of the RxJS library. Observables provide a way to handle asynchronous data streams, making it easy to react to data changes and manage events.

4.4.2.1 Understanding Observables

Observables allow you to subscribe to data streams and receive notifications whenever new data is available. When you call a method from the HttpClient, such as get(), it returns an observable.

Example of subscribing to an observable:

```typescript
typescript
Copy code
this.taskService.getTasks().subscribe(tasks => {
  this.tasks = tasks;
});
```

In this example:

- getTasks() returns an observable that emits the list of tasks.
- The subscribe() method is used to listen for emitted values, updating the tasks property in the component.

4.4.3 Displaying Fetched Data in the Template

Now that we have the data available in our component, let's display it in the template. We've already set up the basic structure for our task list, but let's ensure it's well-presented.

4.4.3.1 Updating the Task Template

Here's a simple way to structure the HTML in task.component.html to display the list of tasks dynamically:

```html
html
Copy code
<h1>Task Manager</h1>

<input [(ngModel)]="newTask" placeholder="Enter a task">
<button (click)="addTask()">Add Task</button>

<h2>Task List</h2>
<ul>
  <li *ngFor="let task of tasks">
    <span [class.completed]="task.isCompleted">{{ task.task
    }}</span>
    <button (click)="removeTask(task.id)">Remove</button>
  </li>
```

```
</ul>
```

In this template:

- The *ngFor directive iterates over the tasks array and creates a list item for each task.
- The completed class can be styled to visually indicate which tasks are completed.

4.4.3.2 Adding CSS Styles

You can enhance the presentation by adding some basic styles in task.component.css:

```css
Copy code
.completed {
    text-decoration: line-through;
    color: grey;
}
```

This style will visually distinguish completed tasks by striking them through and changing their color to grey.

4.4.4 Testing the Full Integration

Now that everything is set up, you can run your Angular application and test the full integration:

1. Ensure your ASP.NET Core API is running.
2. Start your Angular application using:

```bash
Copy code
ng serve
```

1. Navigate to http://localhost:4200 in your web browser. You should see your task manager interface, where you can add and remove tasks, and any changes will be reflected in real-time.

Conclusion

In this chapter, you learned how to connect your Angular frontend with your ASP.NET Core backend by creating and consuming RESTful APIs. We explored how to make API calls from Angular, handle CORS configuration, and display data from the backend in your Angular application.

Chapter 5: Working with Databases in ASP.NET Core

D atabases play a crucial role in modern web applications, providing a structured way to store, retrieve, and manipulate data. In this chapter, we will explore how to integrate databases with your ASP.NET Core application using Entity Framework Core (EF Core). We'll cover how to set up your database context, perform database migrations, and implement CRUD operations to interact with your data effectively.

Understanding Entity Framework Core

5.1.1 What is Entity Framework Core?

Entity Framework Core (EF Core) is a lightweight, extensible, and cross-platform version of Entity Framework, designed specifically for .NET Core applications. EF Core is an Object-Relational Mapper (ORM), which means it enables developers to work with relational databases using .NET objects. This abstraction simplifies database interactions, allowing you to focus on your application's business logic rather than writing raw SQL queries.

5.1.1.1 Key Features of EF Core

EF Core comes with several features that make it a powerful tool for database management:

- **Code-First Approach**: You can define your database schema using C# classes, and EF Core will create the database for you.
- **LINQ Queries**: EF Core allows you to write queries using LINQ (Language Integrated Query), which provides a strongly typed way to query data.
- **Change Tracking**: EF Core automatically tracks changes made to your entities, making it easy to persist updates back to the database.
- **Migrations**: EF Core provides a mechanism for managing database schema changes over time, allowing you to keep your database in sync with your application's data model.

5.1.2 Setting Up Entity Framework Core in ASP.NET Core

Before you can start using EF Core, you need to set it up in your ASP.NET Core application. This involves installing the necessary packages and configuring your database context.

5.1.2.1 Installing EF Core Packages

To use EF Core, you need to install the appropriate NuGet packages. Open your terminal and navigate to your ASP.NET Core project directory, then run the following commands:

For SQL Server:

```
bash
Copy code
dotnet add package Microsoft.EntityFrameworkCore.SqlServer
dotnet add package Microsoft.EntityFrameworkCore.Tools
```

For SQLite (if you prefer a lightweight database):

```
bash
Copy code
dotnet add package Microsoft.EntityFrameworkCore.Sqlite
dotnet add package Microsoft.EntityFrameworkCore.Tools
```

These packages provide the core functionality needed to work with the specified database type.

5.1.2.2 Creating the Database Context

The database context is the primary class that manages the database connection and provides access to the entities. Create a new folder called Data in your project, and inside this folder, create a new class called AppDbContext.cs.

Here's an example of what your AppDbContext might look like:

```csharp
Copy code
using Microsoft.EntityFrameworkCore;
using FullStackApp.Models;

namespace FullStackApp.Data
{
    public class AppDbContext : DbContext
    {
        public AppDbContext(DbContextOptions<AppDbContext>
        options) : base(options) { }

        public DbSet<TaskModel> Tasks { get; set; }
    }
}
```

In this example:

- AppDbContext inherits from DbContext, which is the base class for interacting with a database in EF Core.
- The constructor takes DbContextOptions<AppDbContext>, which allows you to configure the database connection string.
- The DbSet<TaskModel> property represents the tasks table in the database.

5.1.2.3 Configuring the Database Context in Startup.cs

Next, you need to configure your database context in the Startup.cs file. Open Startup.cs and modify the ConfigureServices method to include the following:

```csharp
Copy code
using Microsoft.EntityFrameworkCore;
using FullStackApp.Data;

public void ConfigureServices
(IServiceCollection services)
{
    services.AddControllers();

    // Configure SQL Server (or use SQLite)
    services.AddDbContext<AppDbContext>
(options =>
        options.UseSqlServer
(Configuration
.GetConnectionString
("DefaultConnection")));

    // Uncomment this for SQLite
    // services.AddDbContext<AppDbContext>(options =>
    //     options.UseSqlite("Data Source=app.db"));
}
```

Make sure to add the connection string to your appsettings.json file:

```json
Copy code
{
  "ConnectionStrings": {
    "DefaultConnection": "Server=
(localdb)\\mssqllocaldb
;Database=FullStackAppDB;
Trusted_Connection=True;"
  }
}
```

5.1.3 Creating the Database and Performing Migrations

Once you have set up the database context, the next step is to create the database and configure it using migrations. Migrations in EF Core provide a way to update the database schema without losing existing data.

5.1.3.1 Creating the Initial Migration

To create your first migration, open your terminal and run the following command:

```bash
Copy code
dotnet ef migrations add InitialCreate
```

This command will generate a migration script based on the current model defined in your AppDbContext. You'll find a new folder called Migrations in your project, containing a new migration class.

5.1.3.2 Applying the Migration to the Database

After creating the migration, you need to apply it to the database. Run the following command:

```bash
Copy code
dotnet ef database update
```

This command applies the migration and creates the database schema in your database.

5.1.3.3 Updating the Model and Adding More Migrations

As your application evolves, you may need to update your data model. To do this, modify the TaskModel class or add new models. After making changes, you can create additional migrations using the same command as before:

```bash
bash
Copy code
dotnet ef migrations add <MigrationName>
```

Remember to apply the migration with:

```bash
bash
Copy code
dotnet ef database update
```

This process helps you manage your database schema effectively throughout the development lifecycle.

Implementing CRUD Operations

With EF Core set up and the database created, you can now implement CRUD operations to interact with the database. CRUD stands for Create, Read, Update, and Delete, and these operations are fundamental to managing data in any application.

5.2.1 Implementing Create Operation

The Create operation involves adding new records to the database. We already set up the AddTask() method in the TasksController to handle this functionality. Let's ensure it's working as intended.

5.2.1.1 Adding a New Task

Here's the AddTask() method in TasksController.cs:

```csharp
csharp
Copy code
[HttpPost]
public ActionResult<TaskModel> AddTask(TaskModel task)
{
```

```
_context.Tasks.Add(task);
_context.SaveChanges();
return CreatedAtAction(nameof(GetTasks), new { id = task.Id },
task);
}
```

In this code:

- The incoming task model is added to the database context.
- SaveChanges() is called to persist the changes to the database.
- A 201 Created response is returned, along with the newly created task.

5.2.2 Implementing Read Operation

The Read operation involves retrieving records from the database. You have already seen the GetTasks() method in TasksController that retrieves the list of tasks.

5.2.2.1 Retrieving All Tasks

Here's how the GetTasks() method looks:

```csharp
Copy code
[HttpGet]
public ActionResult<IEnumerable<TaskModel>> GetTasks()
{
    var tasks = _context.Tasks.ToList();
    return Ok(tasks);
}
```

This method uses the database context to fetch all tasks and returns them as a JSON response.

5.2.2.2 Retrieving a Task by ID

To implement fetching a single task by its ID, you can add the following method in TasksController:

65

```csharp
Copy code
[HttpGet("{id}")]
public ActionResult<TaskModel> GetTaskById(int id)
{
    var task = _context.Tasks.Find(id);
    if (task == null)
    {
        return NotFound();
    }
    return Ok(task);
}
```

In this method:

- The task is retrieved using the Find() method, which looks for an entity with the specified primary key.
- If the task does not exist, a 404 Not Found response is returned.

5.2.3 Implementing Update Operation

The Update operation involves modifying existing records in the database. This can be implemented in the controller as follows.

5.2.3.1 Updating a Task

You can create an UpdateTask() method in TasksController:

```csharp
Copy code
[HttpPut("{id}")]
public IActionResult UpdateTask(int id, TaskModel updatedTask)
{
    var task = _context.Tasks.Find(id);
    if (task == null)
    {
        return NotFound();
```

```
    }

    task.Task = updatedTask.Task; // Update properties as needed
    task.IsCompleted = updatedTask.IsCompleted;
    _context.SaveChanges();

    return NoContent();
}
```

In this method:

- The existing task is fetched from the database.
- The properties of the task are updated with the values from the updated-Task parameter.
- Changes are persisted with SaveChanges().

5.2.4 Implementing Delete Operation

The Delete operation involves removing records from the database. The DeleteTask() method handles this functionality.

5.2.4.1 Deleting a Task

Here's how the DeleteTask() method looks:

```csharp
Copy code
[HttpDelete("{id}")]
public IActionResult DeleteTask(int id)
{
    var task = _context.Tasks.Find(id);
    if (task == null)
    {
        return NotFound();
    }

    _context.Tasks.Remove(task);
    _context.SaveChanges();
```

```
    return NoContent();
}
```

In this method:

- The task is retrieved using Find().
- If found, it is removed from the database context.
- Changes are saved to persist the deletion.

5.2.5 Testing CRUD Operations

With all CRUD operations implemented, you can test them using tools like Postman or directly from your Angular application.

1. **Creating a Task**: Send a POST request to /api/tasks with a JSON body containing the task data.
2. **Reading Tasks**: Send a GET request to /api/tasks to retrieve all tasks or /api/tasks/{id} to get a specific task.
3. **Updating a Task**: Send a PUT request to /api/tasks/{id} with updated task data in the body.
4. **Deleting a Task**: Send a DELETE request to /api/tasks/{id} to remove a specific task.

Conclusion

In this chapter, you learned how to work with databases in your ASP.NET Core application using Entity Framework Core. We covered the fundamentals of EF Core, how to set up your database context, and how to implement CRUD operations to interact with your data.

Chapter 6: Implementing User Authentication and Authorization

U ser authentication and authorization are crucial components of modern web applications. This chapter will guide you through implementing a robust authentication and authorization system in your ASP.NET Core backend and integrating it with your Angular frontend. By the end of this chapter, you will have a solid understanding of how to manage user identities, secure your API endpoints, and protect your application from unauthorized access.

Understanding Authentication and Authorization

6.1.1 What is Authentication?

Authentication is the process of verifying the identity of a user or application. In a web application, authentication usually involves users providing credentials (like a username and password) to gain access. If the provided credentials are valid, the user is considered authenticated.

6.1.2 What is Authorization?

Authorization occurs after authentication and determines what an authenticated user is allowed to do within the application. This might include accessing certain resources, performing specific actions, or viewing particular pages. Authorization ensures that users have the correct permissions for their roles.

6.1.3 Key Concepts in Authentication and Authorization

- **Credentials**: Information used to verify identity, such as usernames, passwords, and security tokens.
- **Tokens**: A common method of maintaining session state in web applications. JWTs are a popular choice for stateless authentication.
- **Roles**: Defines the different levels of access within the application (e.g., admin, user, guest).
- **Claims**: A key-value pair that contains information about the user, such as their role or permissions.

Setting Up Authentication in ASP.NET Core

6.2.1 Installing Required Packages

To implement authentication in ASP.NET Core, you need to install several NuGet packages. Open your terminal and navigate to your ASP.NET Core project directory, then run the following commands:

```bash
Copy code
dotnet add package Microsoft.AspNetCore.Authentication.JwtBearer
dotnet add package
Microsoft.AspNetCore.Identity.EntityFrameworkCore
dotnet add package Microsoft.EntityFrameworkCore.SqlServer
```

These packages will enable JWT authentication and integrate Identity services into your application.

6.2.2 Configuring Identity in ASP.NET Core

ASP.NET Core Identity is a membership system that adds user management functionality to your application. This system provides user registration, password recovery, role management, and more.

6.2.2.1 Creating the Application User Class

Create a new class called ApplicationUser.cs in the Models folder that extends the IdentityUser class:

```csharp
Copy code
using Microsoft.AspNetCore.Identity;

namespace FullStackApp.Models
{
    public class ApplicationUser : IdentityUser
    {
        // You can add additional properties here if needed
    }
}
```

6.2.2.2 Setting Up the Database Context for Identity

Next, modify the AppDbContext to use Identity. Open AppDbContext.cs and add the following:

```csharp
Copy code
using Microsoft.AspNetCore.Identity.
EntityFrameworkCore;

namespace FullStackApp.Data
{
```

```
    public class AppDbContext :
IdentityDbContext<ApplicationUser>
    {
        public AppDbContext(DbContextOptions
<AppDbContext> options) : base(options) { }

        public DbSet<TaskModel> Tasks { get; set; }
    }
}
```

In this example, the AppDbContext class now inherits from IdentityDbCont ext<ApplicationUser>, which includes all the necessary tables for Identity.

6.2.2.3 Configuring Identity Services in Startup.cs

In the Startup.cs file, you need to configure Identity services. Update the ConfigureServices method as follows:

```
csharp
Copy code
using Microsoft.AspNetCore.Identity;

public void ConfigureServices
(IServiceCollection services)
{
    services.AddDbContext<AppDbContext>(options =>
        options.UseSqlServer(Configuration.
GetConnectionString("DefaultConnection")));

    services.AddIdentity<ApplicationUser, IdentityRole>()
.AddEntityFrameworkStores<AppDbContext>()
.AddDefaultTokenProviders();

    services.AddControllers();

    // Configure JWT Authentication
    services.AddAuthentication(options =>
    {
        options.DefaultAuthenticateScheme =
```

```
        JwtBearerDefaults.AuthenticationScheme;
        options.DefaultChallengeScheme =
        JwtBearerDefaults.AuthenticationScheme;
    })
    .AddJwtBearer(options =>
    {
        options.TokenValidationParameters = new
        TokenValidationParameters
        {
            ValidateIssuer = true,
            ValidateAudience = true,
            ValidateLifetime = true,
            ValidateIssuerSigningKey = true,
            ValidIssuer = Configuration["Jwt:Issuer"],
ValidAudience = Configuration["Jwt:Audience"],
IssuerSigningKey = new
SymmetricSecurityKey(Encoding.UTF8.
GetBytes(Configuration["Jwt:Key"]))
        };
    });
}
```

6.2.3 Setting Up JWT Authentication

JSON Web Tokens (JWT) are a popular method for securely transmitting information between parties. They are stateless and can carry claims about the user.

6.2.3.1 Creating JWT Settings in appsettings.json

You need to define JWT settings in your appsettings.json file:

```json
Copy code
"Jwt": {
    "Key": "YourSuperSecretKey",
    "Issuer": "YourAppName",
    "Audience": "YourAppUsers"
```

73

```
}
```

Make sure to replace YourSuperSecretKey with a strong secret key.

6.2.3.2 Generating JWT Tokens

Create a service to generate JWT tokens. Create a new file called TokenService.cs in the Services folder:

```csharp
csharp
Copy code
using Microsoft.IdentityModel.Tokens;
using System;
using System.IdentityModel.Tokens.Jwt;
using System.Security.Claims;
using System.Text;

namespace FullStackApp.Services
{
    public class TokenService
    {
        private readonly string _key;
        private readonly string _issuer;
        private readonly string _audience;

        public TokenService(string key, string issuer, string
        audience)
        {
            _key = key;
            _issuer = issuer;
            _audience = audience;
        }

        public string GenerateToken(ApplicationUser user)
        {
            var claims = new[]
            {
                new Claim(ClaimTypes.NameIdentifier, user.Id),
                new Claim(ClaimTypes.Name, user.UserName)
            };
```

```
var key = new
SymmetricSecurityKey(Encoding.UTF8.GetBytes(_key));
var creds = new SigningCredentials(key,
SecurityAlgorithms.HmacSha256);

var token = new JwtSecurityToken(
    _issuer,
    _audience,
    claims,
    expires: DateTime.Now.AddMinutes(30),
    signingCredentials: creds);

        return new JwtSecurityTokenHandler()
.WriteToken(token);
        }

    }
}
```

This service generates a JWT token when a user successfully logs in.

6.2.4 User Registration and Login

Now that we have set up authentication, let's implement user registration and login functionality.

6.2.4.1 Creating the Account Controller

Create a new controller called AccountController.cs in the Controllers folder:

```csharp
Copy code
using Microsoft.AspNetCore.Identity;
using Microsoft.AspNetCore.Mvc;
using FullStackApp.Models;
using FullStackApp.Services;
```

```
using System.Threading.Tasks;

namespace FullStackApp.Controllers
{
    [Route("api/[controller]")]
    [ApiController]
    public class AccountController : ControllerBase
    {
        private readonly UserManager
<ApplicationUser> _userManager;
        private readonly TokenService
_tokenService;

        public AccountController
(UserManager<ApplicationUser>
userManager, TokenService tokenService)
        {
            _userManager = userManager;
            _tokenService = tokenService;
        }

        [HttpPost("register")]
        public async Task<IActionResult>
Register([FromBody] RegisterModel model)
        {
            var user = new ApplicationUser { UserName =
            model.Username, Email = model.Email };
            var result = await _
userManager.CreateAsync(user, model.Password);
            if (result.Succeeded)
            {
                return Ok();
            }

            return BadRequest(result.Errors);
        }

        [HttpPost("login")]
        public async Task<IActionResult>
Login([FromBody] LoginModel model)
```

```csharp
    {
        var user = await
        _userManager.FindByNameAsync(model.Username);
        if (user == null || !await
        _userManager.CheckPasswordAsync(user, model.Password))
        {
            return Unauthorized();
        }

        var token = _tokenService.GenerateToken(user);
        return Ok(new { Token = token });
    }
  }
}
```

In this controller:

- **Register**: Handles user registration, creating a new user with the provided credentials.
- **Login**: Authenticates the user and returns a JWT token if successful.

6.2.4.2 Creating Models for Registration and Login

Create two simple models called RegisterModel.cs and LoginModel.cs in the Models folder.

RegisterModel.cs:

```csharp
csharp
Copy code
namespace FullStackApp.Models
{
    public class RegisterModel
    {
        public string Username { get; set; }
        public string Email { get; set; }
        public string Password { get; set; }
    }
```

}

LoginModel.cs:

```csharp
Copy code
namespace FullStackApp.Models
{
    public class LoginModel
    {
        public string Username { get; set; }
        public string Password { get; set; }
    }
}
```

Integrating Authentication in Angular

Now that the backend authentication is set up, let's integrate it into the Angular frontend.

6.3.1 Creating the Auth Service

In your Angular project, create a new service called auth.service.ts to handle authentication logic. Use the Angular CLI to generate the service:

```bash
Copy code
ng generate service auth
```

6.3.1.1 Implementing the Auth Service

Open auth.service.ts and implement methods for registration, login, and storing the token:

```typescript
typescript
Copy code
import { Injectable } from '@angular/core';
import { HttpClient } from '@angular/common/http';
import { Observable } from 'rxjs';

@Injectable({
  providedIn: 'root'
})
export class AuthService {
  private apiUrl = 'http://localhost:5000/api/account'; // API URL

  constructor(private http: HttpClient) { }

  register(model: any): Observable<any> {
    return this.http.post(`${this.apiUrl}/register`, model);
  }

  login(model: any): Observable<any> {
    return this.http.post(`${this.apiUrl}/login`, model);
  }

  setToken(token: string): void {
    localStorage.setItem('token', token);
  }

  getToken(): string | null {
    return localStorage.getItem('token');
  }

  isAuthenticated(): boolean {
    const token = this.getToken();
    // Token expiration logic can be added here
    return !!token; // Returns true if token exists
  }

  logout(): void {
    localStorage.removeItem('token');
  }
}
```

6.3.2 Creating Login and Registration Components

Next, create components for user registration and login.

6.3.2.1 Generating the Components

Run the following commands to generate the components:

```bash
Copy code
ng generate component register
ng generate component login
```

6.3.2.2 Implementing the Registration Component

Open register.component.ts and implement the registration logic:

```typescript
Copy code
import { Component } from '@angular/core';
import { AuthService } from '../auth.service';

@Component({
  selector: 'app-register',
  templateUrl: './register.component.html',
  styleUrls: ['./register.component.css']
})
export class RegisterComponent {
  model: any = {};

  constructor(private authService: AuthService) {}

  register() {
    this.authService.register(this.model).subscribe(
      () => {
        console.log('Registration successful');
      },
      error => {
        console.error('Registration failed', error);
      }
    );
```

```
    }
}
```

Implement the template in register.component.html:

```html
Copy code
<h2>Register</h2>
<form (ngSubmit)="register()">
  <input type="text" [(ngModel)]="model.username" name="username"
  placeholder="Username" required>
  <input type="email" [(ngModel)]="model.email" name="email"
  placeholder="Email" required>
  <input type="password" [(ngModel)]="model.password"
  name="password" placeholder="Password" required>
  <button type="submit">Register</button>
</form>
```

6.3.2.3 Implementing the Login Component

Open login.component.ts and implement the login logic:

```typescript
Copy code
import { Component } from '@angular/core';
import { AuthService } from '../auth.service';
import { Router } from '@angular/router';

@Component({
  selector: 'app-login',
  templateUrl: './login.component.html',
  styleUrls: ['./login.component.css']
})
export class LoginComponent {
  model: any = {};

  constructor(private authService: AuthService, private router:
  Router) {}
```

```
login() {
  this.authService.login(this.model).subscribe(
    response => {
      this.authService.setToken(response.token);
      this.router.navigate(['/']);
    },
    error => {
      console.error('Login failed', error);
    }
  );
}
}
```

Implement the template in login.component.html:

```html
Copy code
<h2>Login</h2>
<form (ngSubmit)="login()">
  <input type="text" [(ngModel)]="model.username" name="username"
  placeholder="Username" required>
  <input type="password" [(ngModel)]="model.password"
  name="password" placeholder="Password" required>
  <button type="submit">Login</button>
</form>
```

6.3.3 Protecting Routes with Guards

To protect certain routes in your Angular application and ensure only authenticated users can access them, you can implement route guards.

6.3.3.1 Generating an Auth Guard

Run the following command to create an Auth Guard:

```
bash
Copy code
ng generate guard auth
```

6.3.3.2 Implementing the Auth Guard

Open auth.guard.ts and implement the guard logic:

```typescript
typescript
Copy code
import { Injectable } from '@angular/core';
import { CanActivate, ActivatedRouteSnapshot, RouterStateSnapshot,
Router } from '@angular/router';
import { AuthService } from './auth.service';

@Injectable({
  providedIn: 'root'
})
export class AuthGuard implements CanActivate {

  constructor(private authService: AuthService, private router:
  Router) {}

  canActivate(
    next: ActivatedRouteSnapshot,
    state: RouterStateSnapshot): boolean {
    if (this.authService.isAuthenticated()) {
      return true;
    }
    this.router.navigate(['/login']);
    return false;
  }
}
```

6.3.3.3 Protecting Routes in the App Routing Module

Now, let's protect the routes in your app-routing.module.ts:

```typescript
Copy code
import { NgModule } from '@angular/core';
import { RouterModule, Routes } from '@angular/router';
import { RegisterComponent } from './register/register.component';
import { LoginComponent } from './login/login.component';
import { TaskComponent } from './task/task.component';
import { AuthGuard } from './auth.guard';

const routes: Routes = [
  { path: '', component: TaskComponent, canActivate: [AuthGuard] },
  { path: 'register', component: RegisterComponent },
  { path: 'login', component: LoginComponent }
];

@NgModule({
  imports: [RouterModule.forRoot(routes)],
  exports: [RouterModule]
})
export class AppRoutingModule { }
```

6.3.4 Testing the Authentication Flow

With the authentication and authorization set up, you can now test the entire flow:

1. **Register a User**: Navigate to /register and fill in the registration form.
2. **Log In**: After successful registration, navigate to /login and log in with the registered credentials.
3. **Access Protected Routes**: Try accessing the protected task component to see if the guard works.

Securing API Endpoints

Now that you have set up authentication, it's essential to secure your API endpoints to ensure that only authenticated users can access them.

6.4.1 Securing Controllers with [Authorize] Attribute

In ASP.NET Core, you can use the [Authorize] attribute to secure your API controllers or specific action methods.

6.4.1.1 Securing the Tasks Controller

Modify the TasksController to require authentication for accessing its endpoints:

```csharp
Copy code
using Microsoft.AspNetCore.Authorization;

[Authorize]
[Route("api/[controller]")]
[ApiController]
public class TasksController : ControllerBase
{
    // Your existing code...
}
```

By applying the [Authorize] attribute at the controller level, all actions within this controller require authentication.

6.4.2 Managing User Roles

To implement role-based authorization, you can use roles in ASP.NET Core Identity. You can create roles and assign them to users, allowing you to control access based on the user's role.

6.4.2.1 Creating Roles in the Database

You can create a new service to manage roles. Create a file called

RoleService.cs in the Services folder:

```csharp
Copy code
using Microsoft.AspNetCore.Identity;
using System.Threading.Tasks;

public class RoleService
{
    private readonly RoleManager<IdentityRole> _roleManager;

    public RoleService(RoleManager<IdentityRole> roleManager)
    {
        _roleManager = roleManager;
    }

    public async Task CreateRole(string roleName)
    {
        if (!await _roleManager.RoleExistsAsync(roleName))
        {
            await _roleManager.CreateAsync(new
            IdentityRole(roleName));
        }
    }
}
```

6.4.2.2 Assigning Roles to Users

You can extend the AccountController to include methods for assigning roles to users:

```csharp
Copy code
[HttpPost("assign-role")]
public async Task<IActionResult> AssignRole(string userId, string
role)
{
    var user = await _userManager.FindByIdAsync(userId);
    if (user == null)
    {
```

```
        return NotFound();
    }

    await _userManager.AddToRoleAsync(user, role);
    return Ok();
}
```

6.4.3 Implementing Role-Based Authorization in the Application

Once roles are assigned, you can use the [Authorize(Roles = "Admin")] attribute to restrict access to certain endpoints based on roles.

```csharp
csharp
Copy code
[Authorize(Roles = "Admin")]
[HttpDelete("{id}")]
public IActionResult DeleteTask(int id)
{
    // Deletion logic...
}
```

In this example, only users with the "Admin" role can access the DeleteTask method.

Conclusion

In this chapter, you learned how to implement user authentication and authorization in your ASP.NET Core application. We covered the essentials of setting up Identity, creating JWT tokens, and integrating authentication in your Angular frontend. You also learned how to secure API endpoints and manage user roles.

Authentication and authorization are vital aspects of any web application, ensuring that only authorized users can access certain resources and actions. With this foundational knowledge, you can build secure applications that protect user data and provide a personalized experience.

Chapter 7: Building Real-Time Applications with SignalR

R eal-time applications have become increasingly popular in today's web landscape, allowing for instant communication and interaction between users. In this chapter, we will explore how to implement real-time functionality in your ASP.NET Core and Angular applications using SignalR. We'll cover the basics of SignalR, how to set it up in your ASP.NET Core backend, and how to integrate it with your Angular frontend to build a dynamic, interactive user experience.

Understanding SignalR

7.1.1 What is SignalR?

SignalR is an open-source library for ASP.NET that simplifies the process of adding real-time web functionality to applications. It allows bi-directional communication between the server and clients, meaning that the server can push updates to connected clients instantly.

7.1.1.1 Key Features of SignalR

- **Real-Time Communication**: SignalR enables real-time updates without requiring the client to poll the server for changes.

- **Automatic Reconnection**: SignalR automatically reconnects clients if the connection is lost.
- **Scalability**: SignalR can handle thousands of concurrent connections, making it suitable for high-load applications.
- **Support for Various Transports**: SignalR supports various transport methods, including WebSockets, Server-Sent Events, and Long Polling. It automatically selects the best transport method available.

7.1.2 Use Cases for SignalR

SignalR is particularly useful for applications that require real-time features. Common use cases include:

- **Chat Applications**: Enable users to communicate instantly with each other.
- **Live Notifications**: Push notifications for updates, alerts, or changes.
- **Real-Time Data Feeds**: Display real-time data updates, such as stock prices or sports scores.
- **Collaboration Tools**: Facilitate real-time collaboration in applications, such as document editing or project management.

Setting Up SignalR in ASP.NET Core

7.2.1 Installing SignalR

To use SignalR in your ASP.NET Core application, you need to install the required NuGet package. Open your terminal and run the following command:

```bash
Copy code
dotnet add package Microsoft.AspNetCore.SignalR
```

7.2.2 Configuring SignalR in Startup.cs

After installing SignalR, you need to configure it in your Startup.cs file.

7.2.2.1 Adding SignalR Services

In the ConfigureServices method, add SignalR services to the service container:

```csharp
Copy code
public void ConfigureServices(IServiceCollection services)
{
    services.AddControllers();
    services.AddSignalR();
}
```

7.2.2.2 Configuring SignalR Endpoints

Next, you need to define the SignalR endpoints in the Configure method:

```csharp
Copy code
public void Configure(IApplicationBuilder app, IWebHostEnvironment env)
{
    // Existing middleware

    app.UseRouting();

    app.UseEndpoints(endpoints =>
    {
        endpoints.MapControllers();
        endpoints.MapHub<ChatHub>("/chatHub"); // Define the hub endpoint
    });
}
```

7.2.3 Creating a SignalR Hub

SignalR uses hubs to communicate with clients. A hub is a class that serves as a central point for communication between the server and connected clients. Let's create a simple chat hub.

7.2.3.1 Creating the ChatHub Class

Create a new folder called Hubs in your project, and create a new class called ChatHub.cs:

```csharp
Copy code
using Microsoft.AspNetCore.SignalR;
using System.Threading.Tasks;

namespace FullStackApp.Hubs
{
    public class ChatHub : Hub
    {
        public async Task SendMessage(string user, string message)
        {
            await Clients.All.SendAsync("ReceiveMessage", user,
            message);
        }
    }
}
```

In this ChatHub class:

- The SendMessage method takes a user and a message as parameters and broadcasts the message to all connected clients using Clients.All.SendAsync.

Integrating SignalR in Angular

With SignalR set up in the ASP.NET Core backend, let's integrate it into the Angular frontend.

7.3.1 Installing SignalR Client

You need to install the SignalR client library in your Angular application. Open your terminal in your Angular project directory and run:

```bash
Copy code
npm install @microsoft/signalr
```

7.3.2 Creating a Chat Service

Next, create a service in Angular to handle communication with the SignalR hub.

7.3.2.1 Generating the Chat Service

Use the Angular CLI to generate a new service:

```bash
Copy code
ng generate service chat
```

7.3.2.2 Implementing the Chat Service

Open chat.service.ts and implement the SignalR connection logic:

```typescript
Copy code
import { Injectable } from '@angular/core';
import { HubConnection, HubConnectionBuilder } from
```

```
'@microsoft/signalr';

@Injectable({
  providedIn: 'root'
})
export class ChatService {
  private hubConnection: HubConnection;

  constructor() {
    this.hubConnection = new HubConnectionBuilder()
      .withUrl('http://localhost:5000/chatHub') // URL of your
      SignalR hub
      .build();

    this.startConnection();
  }

  private startConnection() {
    this.hubConnection
      .start()
      .then(() => console.log('Connection started'))
      .catch(err => console.log('Error while starting connection:
      ' + err));
  }

  public sendMessage(user: string, message: string) {
    this.hubConnection.invoke('SendMessage', user, message)
      .catch(err => console.error(err));
  }

  public receiveMessage() {
    return this.hubConnection.on('ReceiveMessage', (user, message)
    => {
      console.log(`${user}: ${message}`);
      // Implement logic to handle received message
    });
  }
}
```

7.3.3 Creating the Chat Component

Next, create a chat component where users can send and receive messages.

7.3.3.1 Generating the Chat Component

Use the Angular CLI to generate the component:

```bash
Copy code
ng generate component chat
```

7.3.3.2 Implementing the Chat Component Logic

Open chat.component.ts and implement the logic for sending and receiving messages:

```typescript
Copy code
import { Component, OnInit } from '@angular/core';
import { ChatService } from '../chat.service';

@Component({
  selector: 'app-chat',
  templateUrl: './chat.component.html',
  styleUrls: ['./chat.component.css']
})
export class ChatComponent implements OnInit {
  public user: string;
  public message: string;
  public messages: string[] = [];

  constructor(private chatService: ChatService) {}

  ngOnInit() {
    this.chatService.receiveMessage().subscribe((user: string,
    message: string) => {
      this.messages.push(`${user}: ${message}`);
    });
  }
```

```
sendMessage() {
  this.chatService.sendMessage(this.user, this.message);
  this.message = '';
}
}
```

7.3.3.3 Implementing the Chat Component Template

Open chat.component.html and implement the UI for sending and displaying messages:

```html
html
Copy code
<h2>Chat Room</h2>
<input [(ngModel)]="user" placeholder="Enter your name">
<input [(ngModel)]="message" placeholder="Type a message">
<button (click)="sendMessage()">Send</button>

<ul>
  <li *ngFor="let msg of messages">{{ msg }}</li>
</ul>
```

7.3.4 Updating Routing to Include the Chat Component

Open app-routing.module.ts and add a route for the chat component:

```typescript
typescript
Copy code
import { ChatComponent } from './chat/chat.component';

const routes: Routes = [
  { path: 'chat', component: ChatComponent },
  // Other routes...
];
```

Testing Real-Time Functionality

With everything set up, it's time to test the real-time chat functionality.

1. **Run the ASP.NET Core backend**: Ensure that your API and SignalR hub are running.
2. **Run the Angular application**: Start your Angular application using ng serve.
3. **Open multiple browser tabs**: Navigate to the chat route (http://localh ost:4200/chat) in multiple tabs to simulate different users.
4. **Test sending messages**: Enter your name and a message in one tab, and click "Send". You should see the message appear in all connected tabs in real-time.

Handling Connection Lifecycle Events

SignalR provides events that allow you to handle various connection states. This section will cover how to manage these events for a better user experience.

7.4.1 Connection Events

You can handle events such as connection start, connection stop, and errors in your chat service.

7.4.1.1 Modifying the Chat Service

Update your ChatService to include connection lifecycle event handling:

```typescript
Copy code
private startConnection() {
  this.hubConnection
    .start()
    .then(() => {
```

```
console.log('Connection started');
this.hubConnection.onclose(() => {
  console.log('Connection closed. Reconnecting...');
  setTimeout(() => this.startConnection(), 5000);
});
})
.catch(err => console.log('Error while starting connection: '
+ err));
}
```

In this modification:

- The onclose event is handled to attempt reconnection if the connection drops.

7.4.2 User Feedback on Connection Status

Providing feedback to users about the connection status can improve the overall experience. You can implement a simple notification system to inform users when they are connected or disconnected.

7.4.2.1 Updating the Chat Component

Modify the ChatComponent to show connection status:

```
typescript
Copy code
public isConnected: boolean = false;

ngOnInit() {
  this.chatService.receiveMessage().subscribe((user: string,
  message: string) => {
    this.messages.push(`${user}: ${message}`);
  });

  this.chatService.hubConnection.on('Connected', () => {
    this.isConnected = true;
  });
```

```
this.chatService.hubConnection.on('Disconnected', () => {
  this.isConnected = false;
});
}
```

7.4.2.2 Displaying Connection Status in the Template

Update the chat.component.html to display connection status:

```html
Copy code
<div *ngIf="isConnected; else disconnected">
  <p>You are connected to the chat!</p>
</div>
<ng-template #disconnected>
  <p>You are disconnected. Please check your internet
  connection.</p>
</ng-template>
```

Securing SignalR Hubs

It's important to secure your SignalR hubs, especially in applications where sensitive data is being transmitted.

7.5.1 Securing the ChatHub

To restrict access to authenticated users, you can apply the [Authorize] attribute to your hub class.

7.5.1.1 Modifying the ChatHub Class

Update your ChatHub class as follows:

```csharp
Copy code
```

```
using Microsoft.AspNetCore.Authorization;

[Authorize]
public class ChatHub : Hub
{
    public async Task SendMessage(string user, string message)
    {
        await Clients.All.SendAsync("ReceiveMessage", user,
        message);
    }
}
```

7.5.2 Handling Authorization in Angular

When sending messages, you must ensure that the user is authenticated. Update the sendMessage method in your ChatService to include the token in the connection options.

7.5.2.1 Modifying the Chat Service for Authorization

```
typescript
Copy code
private startConnection() {
  this.hubConnection = new HubConnectionBuilder()
    .withUrl('http://localhost:5000/chatHub', {
      accessTokenFactory: () => this.authService.getToken() // Use
      the token for authorization
    })
    .build();

  // Existing connection logic...
}
```

By providing the accessTokenFactory, you ensure that the JWT token is sent with the request to connect to the SignalR hub.

Conclusion

In this chapter, you learned how to build real-time applications using SignalR in your ASP.NET Core and Angular stack. We covered the fundamental concepts of SignalR, how to set it up in your ASP.NET Core backend, and how to integrate it into your Angular frontend.

You also explored important aspects such as handling connection lifecycle events, securing your SignalR hubs, and ensuring that only authenticated users can send and receive messages. With this knowledge, you can create dynamic and interactive applications that provide users with real-time features, enhancing the overall user experience.

Chapter 8: Implementing Advanced Features

A s your application grows, implementing advanced features becomes essential to enhance functionality and improve user experience. In this chapter, we will explore how to handle file uploads, send real-time notifications to users, and manage errors effectively in your ASP.NET Core and Angular application. These features will provide your application with the robustness and interactivity that modern users expect.

Handling File Uploads in ASP.NET Core

8.1.1 Introduction to File Uploads

File uploads are a common feature in web applications, allowing users to send files (images, documents, etc.) to the server for processing or storage. In ASP.NET Core, handling file uploads is straightforward, thanks to its built-in support for file management.

8.1.2 Configuring File Uploads

8.1.2.1 Setting Up the Model

First, let's create a model to represent the uploaded file. Create a new class called FileUploadModel.cs in the Models folder:

```csharp
Copy code
namespace FullStackApp.Models
{
    public class FileUploadModel
    {
        public string FileName { get; set; }
        public string ContentType { get; set; }
        public long Size { get; set; }
    }
}
```

This model will help us track information about the uploaded files.

8.1.2.2 Creating the File Upload Controller

Next, create a controller that handles file uploads. Create a new controller called FileUploadController.cs in the Controllers folder:

```csharp
Copy code
using Microsoft.AspNetCore.Http;
using Microsoft.AspNetCore.Mvc;
using System.IO;
using System.Threading.Tasks;

namespace FullStackApp.Controllers
{
    [Route("api/[controller]")]
    [ApiController]
    public class FileUploadController : ControllerBase
    {
        private readonly string _storagePath =
```

```
Path.Combine(Directory.GetCurrentDirectory(),
"UploadedFiles");

public FileUploadController()
{
    if (!Directory.Exists(_storagePath))
    {
        Directory.CreateDirectory(_storagePath);
    }
}

[HttpPost]
public async Task<IActionResult> UploadFile(IFormFile file)
{
    if (file == null || file.Length == 0)
        return BadRequest("No file uploaded.");

    var filePath = Path.Combine(_storagePath,
    file.FileName);

    using (var stream = new FileStream(filePath,
    FileMode.Create))
    {
        await file.CopyToAsync(stream);
    }

    var fileUploadModel = new FileUploadModel
    {
        FileName = file.FileName,
        ContentType = file.ContentType,
        Size = file.Length
    };

    return Ok(fileUploadModel);
    }
  }
}
```

In this controller:

- The UploadFile method takes an IFormFile parameter, which represents the uploaded file.
- The method checks if the file is valid, saves it to a designated directory, and returns information about the uploaded file.

8.1.3 Configuring the Angular Frontend for File Uploads

With the backend ready to handle file uploads, let's create a frontend component that allows users to upload files.

8.1.3.1 Generating the File Upload Component

Use the Angular CLI to generate a new component:

```bash
Copy code
ng generate component file-upload
```

8.1.3.2 Implementing the File Upload Logic

Open file-upload.component.ts and implement the file upload logic:

```typescript
Copy code
import { Component } from '@angular/core';
import { HttpClient } from '@angular/common/http';

@Component({
  selector: 'app-file-upload',
  templateUrl: './file-upload.component.html',
  styleUrls: ['./file-upload.component.css']
})
export class FileUploadComponent {
  selectedFile: File | null = null;

  constructor(private http: HttpClient) {}

  onFileSelected(event: any) {
```

```
    this.selectedFile = event.target.files[0];
  }

  uploadFile() {
    if (this.selectedFile) {
      const formData = new FormData();
      formData.append('file', this.selectedFile,
      this.selectedFile.name);

      this.http.post('http://localhost:5000/api/fileupload',
      formData)
        .subscribe(response => {
          console.log('File uploaded successfully', response);
        }, error => {
          console.error('Error uploading file', error);
        });
    }
  }
}
```

In this component:

- The onFileSelected method captures the file selected by the user.
- The uploadFile method creates a FormData object and appends the selected file before sending a POST request to the backend.

8.1.3.3 Implementing the File Upload Template

Open file-upload.component.html and implement the upload UI:

```html
Copy code
<h2>File Upload</h2>
<input type="file" (change)="onFileSelected($event)">
<button (click)="uploadFile()">Upload</button>
```

8.1.4 Testing the File Upload Functionality

To test the file upload functionality:

1. Start your ASP.NET Core backend.
2. Run your Angular application.
3. Navigate to the file upload component.
4. Select a file and click "Upload". You should see a success message in the console, and the file will be saved on the server.

Sending Real-Time Notifications with SignalR

Notifications are an essential feature in many applications, informing users about various events or updates. In this section, we will implement real-time notifications using SignalR, building upon the SignalR setup from Chapter 7.

8.2.1 Understanding Notifications in SignalR

SignalR enables you to send messages to connected clients instantly. This can be useful for notifications such as:

- New messages in a chat application.
- System alerts for users.
- Updates on file uploads or processing.

8.2.2 Implementing Notification Logic in the Chat Hub

We will extend the existing ChatHub to include notification functionality.
8.2.2.1 Modifying the ChatHub Class
Open ChatHub.cs and add a method for sending notifications:

```csharp
Copy code
public async Task SendNotification(string message)
{
    await Clients.All.SendAsync("ReceiveNotification", message);
}
```

8.2.3 Sending Notifications from the File Upload Controller

To send notifications when a file is successfully uploaded, modify the FileUploadController to include the IHubContext<ChatHub> service.

8.2.3.1 Injecting Hub Context

Update the FileUploadController constructor:

```csharp
Copy code
private readonly IHubContext<ChatHub> _hubContext;

public FileUploadController(IHubContext<ChatHub> hubContext)
{
    _hubContext = hubContext;
    // Existing initialization code...
}
```

8.2.3.2 Sending Notifications Upon Successful File Upload

Modify the UploadFile method to send a notification:

```csharp
Copy code
[HttpPost]
public async Task<IActionResult> UploadFile(IFormFile file)
{
    // Existing upload logic...

    // Send notification
    await _hubContext.Clients.All.SendAsync("ReceiveNotification",
```

```
$"{file.FileName} has been uploaded.");

    return Ok(fileUploadModel);
}
```

8.2.4 Receiving Notifications in Angular

To receive notifications in the Angular frontend, we will extend the chat service.

8.2.4.1 Updating the Chat Service
Modify chat.service.ts to include notification handling:

```typescript
Copy code
public receiveNotification() {
    this.hubConnection.on('ReceiveNotification', (message: string)
    => {
        console.log('Notification:', message);
        // Implement logic to display notifications to users
    });
}
```

8.2.4.2 Updating the Chat Component
Open chat.component.ts and subscribe to notifications:

```typescript
Copy code
ngOnInit() {
    // Existing message reception logic...

    this.chatService.receiveNotification();
}
```

8.2.5 Displaying Notifications

You can implement a notification display mechanism in the chat component.

8.2.5.1 Updating the Chat Component Template

Add a section in chat.component.html to display notifications:

```html
Copy code
<h2>Notifications</h2>
<div *ngFor="let notification of notifications">{{ notification }}</div>
```

8.2.5.2 Updating the Chat Component Logic

Add a notifications array in chat.component.ts:

```typescript
Copy code
public notifications: string[] = [];

this.chatService.receiveNotification().subscribe(message => {
    this.notifications.push(message);
});
```

Implementing Robust Error Handling

Error handling is crucial in any application to ensure a good user experience. In this section, we will implement robust error handling in both the ASP.NET Core backend and the Angular frontend.

8.3.1 Error Handling in ASP.NET Core

8.3.1.1 Global Exception Handling Middleware

You can create middleware to handle exceptions globally in your ASP.NET Core application. Create a new class called ErrorHandlingMiddleware.cs:

```csharp
Copy code
using Microsoft.AspNetCore.Http;
using System;
using System.Net;
using System.Threading.Tasks;

public class ErrorHandlingMiddleware
{
    private readonly RequestDelegate _next;

    public ErrorHandlingMiddleware(RequestDelegate next)
    {
        _next = next;
    }

    public async Task Invoke(HttpContext context)
    {
        try
        {
            await _next(context);
        }
        catch (Exception ex)
        {
            await HandleExceptionAsync(context, ex);
        }
    }

    private Task HandleExceptionAsync(HttpContext context,
    Exception ex)
    {
        context.Response.ContentType = "application/json";
        context.Response.StatusCode =
        (int)HttpStatusCode.InternalServerError;

        return context.Response.WriteAsync(new
        {
            StatusCode = context.Response.StatusCode,
```

```
        Message = "Internal Server Error",
        Detailed = ex.Message // Include more detailed error
        information as needed
    }.ToString());
    }
}
```

8.3.1.2 Registering the Middleware

Register the error handling middleware in the Configure method of Startup.cs:

```csharp
csharp
Copy code
public void Configure(IApplicationBuilder app, IWebHostEnvironment env)
{
    app.UseMiddleware<ErrorHandlingMiddleware>();

    // Existing middleware...
}
```

8.3.2 Error Handling in Angular

Handling errors in Angular involves intercepting HTTP responses and managing error messages.

8.3.2.1 Creating an Interceptor

Create an interceptor that will handle HTTP errors. Use the Angular CLI to generate an interceptor:

```bash
bash
Copy code
ng generate interceptor error
```

8.3.2.2 Implementing the Error Interceptor

Open error.interceptor.ts and implement error handling logic:

```typescript
Copy code
import { Injectable } from '@angular/core';
import { HttpEvent, HttpInterceptor, HttpHandler, HttpRequest,
HttpErrorResponse } from '@angular/common/http';
import { Observable, throwError } from 'rxjs';
import { catchError } from 'rxjs/operators';

@Injectable()
export class ErrorInterceptor implements HttpInterceptor {
  intercept(req: HttpRequest<any>, next: HttpHandler):
  Observable<HttpEvent<any>> {
    return next.handle(req).pipe(
      catchError((error: HttpErrorResponse) => {
        let errorMessage = '';
        if (error.error instanceof ErrorEvent) {
          // Client-side error
          errorMessage = `Error: ${error.error.message}`;
        } else {
          // Server-side error
          errorMessage = `Error Code: ${error.status}\nMessage:
          ${error.message}`;
        }
        console.error(errorMessage);
        return throwError(errorMessage);
      })
    );
  }
}
```

8.3.2.3 Registering the Interceptor

Update the app.module.ts to provide the interceptor:

```typescript
Copy code
import { HTTP_INTERCEPTORS } from '@angular/common/http';
import { ErrorInterceptor } from './error.interceptor';
```

```
@NgModule({
  providers: [
    { provide: HTTP_INTERCEPTORS, useClass: ErrorInterceptor,
    multi: true }
  ],
})
export class AppModule { }
```

8.3.3 Displaying Error Messages in Angular

You can enhance the user experience by displaying error messages in the UI.

8.3.3.1 Updating the Chat Component

Modify the chat.component.ts to handle error notifications:

```typescript
Copy code
public errorMessage: string;

this.chatService.login(this.model).subscribe(
  response => {
    // Handle success...
  },
  error => {
    this.errorMessage = error;
  }
);
```

8.3.3.2 Displaying Error Messages in the Template

Update chat.component.html to show error messages:

```html
Copy code
<div *ngIf="errorMessage" class="error">{{ errorMessage }}</div>
```

Conclusion

In this chapter, you learned how to implement advanced features in your ASP.NET Core and Angular application, including handling file uploads, sending real-time notifications with SignalR, and implementing robust error handling.

By integrating file uploads, you enhanced your application's capabilities to handle user-generated content. Real-time notifications allowed for immediate feedback to users, improving the interactivity of your application. Lastly, robust error handling ensures that users have a smooth experience, even when things go wrong.

Chapter 9: Implementing Unit Testing and End-to-End Testing

T esting is a critical aspect of software development, ensuring that your application behaves as expected and meets user requirements. In this chapter, we will explore how to implement unit testing and end-to-end (E2E) testing in your ASP.NET Core and Angular applications. By the end of this chapter, you will have a solid understanding of testing frameworks, tools, and best practices to ensure the quality and reliability of your applications.

Understanding Testing

9.1.1 What is Unit Testing?

Unit testing involves testing individual components or functions in isolation to verify that they work as intended. A unit test typically targets a single "unit" of code, such as a method or function, and checks for correct output given a specific input. Unit tests help catch bugs early in the development process and provide a safety net for refactoring code.

9.1.1.1 Benefits of Unit Testing

- **Early Bug Detection**: Identifies bugs before the code is integrated into larger components.

- **Simplifies Integration**: Makes it easier to integrate components, as each unit is verified to work independently.
- **Facilitates Refactoring**: Allows developers to change and improve code with confidence, knowing that tests will catch any introduced errors.
- **Documentation**: Serves as documentation for the code, helping new developers understand the expected behavior of functions.

9.1.2 What is End-to-End Testing?

End-to-end (E2E) testing involves testing the entire application flow from start to finish, simulating real user scenarios. E2E tests verify that the integrated components work together as expected and that the application meets business requirements.

9.1.2.1 Benefits of End-to-End Testing

- **Comprehensive Validation**: Ensures that all parts of the application work together correctly.
- **User-Centric Testing**: Tests user journeys, verifying that the application behaves as expected from the user's perspective.
- **Reduces Regression Bugs**: Helps catch issues that arise from changes in different parts of the application.

Unit Testing in ASP.NET Core

9.2.1 Setting Up a Testing Project

To implement unit testing in your ASP.NET Core application, you need to create a separate testing project.

9.2.1.1 Creating a Test Project

In your solution directory, run the following command to create a new test project:

```bash
bash
Copy code
dotnet new xunit -n FullStackApp.Tests
```

This command creates a new xUnit test project named FullStackApp.Tests.

9.2.1.2 Adding References to the Main Project

Navigate to the newly created test project directory and add a reference to your main ASP.NET Core project:

```bash
bash
Copy code
cd FullStackApp.Tests
dotnet add reference ../FullStackApp/FullStackApp.csproj
```

9.2.2 Writing Unit Tests

9.2.2.1 Installing Necessary Packages

Ensure you have the necessary packages installed in your test project. Open the terminal in your test project directory and run:

```bash
bash
Copy code
dotnet add package Moq
dotnet add package FluentAssertions
```

- **Moq**: A popular library for creating mock objects in unit tests.
- **FluentAssertions**: A library that makes it easier to write readable assertions in tests.

9.2.2.2 Writing a Simple Unit Test

Create a new folder called Controllers in your test project, and add a test class for the TasksController.

TasksControllerTests.cs:

```csharp
csharp
Copy code
using FluentAssertions;
using Microsoft.AspNetCore.Mvc;
using Moq;
using Xunit;

namespace FullStackApp.Tests.Controllers
{
    public class TasksControllerTests
    {
        private readonly TasksController _controller;
        private readonly Mock<IRepository<TaskModel>>
        _mockRepository;

        public TasksControllerTests()
        {
            _mockRepository = new Mock<IRepository<TaskModel>>();
            _controller = new
            TasksController(_mockRepository.Object);
        }

        [Fact]
        public void GetTasks_ReturnsOkResult_WhenTasksExist()
        {
            // Arrange
            _mockRepository.Setup(repo =>
            repo.GetAll()).Returns(GetTestTasks());

            // Act
            var result = _controller.GetTasks();

            // Assert
            result.Should().BeOfType<OkObjectResult>();
        }

        private List<TaskModel> GetTestTasks()
        {
```

```
        return new List<TaskModel>
        {
            new TaskModel { Id = 1, Task = "Learn ASP.NET
            Core", IsCompleted = false },
            new TaskModel { Id = 2, Task = "Learn Angular",
            IsCompleted = false }
        };
    }
}
}
```

In this example:

- The TasksControllerTests class sets up a mock repository and the controller instance for testing.
- The GetTasks_ReturnsOkResult_WhenTasksExist test verifies that the controller returns an OkObjectResult when tasks are present.

9.2.3 Running Unit Tests

To run your unit tests, navigate to the test project directory and execute the following command:

```
bash
Copy code
dotnet test
```

This command will build the test project and execute all tests, displaying the results in the console.

Unit Testing in Angular

9.3.1 Setting Up Angular Testing

Angular projects come with built-in support for testing using Jasmine and Karma.

9.3.1.1 Understanding Testing Frameworks

- **Jasmine**: A behavior-driven development framework for testing JavaScript code.
- **Karma**: A test runner that allows you to run tests in real browsers.

9.3.2 Writing Unit Tests in Angular

9.3.2.1 Generating a Test File

When you generate a component using Angular CLI, a corresponding test file (.spec.ts) is created automatically. You can find this file in the same directory as the component.

9.3.2.2 Writing Unit Tests for the Chat Component

Open chat.component.spec.ts and add tests for your chat component:

```typescript
Copy code
import { ComponentFixture, TestBed } from '@angular/core/testing';
import { ChatComponent } from './chat.component';
import { ChatService } from '../chat.service';
import { of } from 'rxjs';

describe('ChatComponent', () => {
  let component: ChatComponent;
  let fixture: ComponentFixture<ChatComponent>;
  let chatService: jasmine.SpyObj<ChatService>;

  beforeEach(() => {
    chatService = jasmine.createSpyObj('ChatService',
    ['sendMessage', 'receiveMessage']);
```

```
TestBed.configureTestingModule({
  declarations: [ChatComponent],
  providers: [{ provide: ChatService, useValue: chatService }]
}).compileComponents();

fixture = TestBed.createComponent(ChatComponent);
component = fixture.componentInstance;
});

it('should send a message', () => {
  component.user = 'User1';
  component.message = 'Hello World';

  chatService.sendMessage.and.returnValue(of(null)); // Mocking
  sendMessage
  component.sendMessage();

  expect(chatService.sendMessage).toHaveBeenCalledWith(component.user,
  component.message);
  expect(component.message).toBe('');
});
});
```

In this example:

- We use jasmine.createSpyObj to create a mock of the ChatService.
- The test verifies that the sendMessage method is called with the correct parameters.

9.3.3 Running Angular Unit Tests

To run your Angular unit tests, use the following command:

```bash
Copy code
ng test
```

This command will launch Karma and run all the tests, providing feedback in the browser.

End-to-End Testing in Angular

9.4.1 Setting Up E2E Testing

Angular provides a built-in framework for E2E testing using Protractor.

9.4.1.1 Understanding Protractor

Protractor is an end-to-end testing framework for Angular applications. It is built on top of WebDriverJS and is designed specifically for Angular apps, automatically waiting for Angular to finish loading before running tests.

9.4.2 Writing E2E Tests

9.4.2.1 Generating an E2E Test File

When you create a new Angular project, an E2E testing configuration is included. You can find the E2E test files in the e2e folder.

9.4.2.2 Writing E2E Tests for the Chat Component

Open app.e2e-spec.ts in the e2e folder and add tests for your chat component:

```typescript
Copy code
import { browser, by, element } from 'protractor';

describe('Chat App E2E Tests', () => {
  it('should display chat messages', async () => {
    await browser.get('/chat'); // Navigate to the chat route

    const userInput = element(by.css('input[placeholder="Enter
    your name"]'));
    const messageInput = element(by.css('input[placeholder="Type a
    message"]'));
    const sendButton = element(by.buttonText('Send'));
```

```
await userInput.sendKeys('User1');
await messageInput.sendKeys('Hello World');
await sendButton.click();

const message = element(by.cssContainingText('li', 'User1:
Hello World'));
expect(await message.isPresent()).toBe(true);
  });
});
```

In this example:

- We navigate to the chat route, simulate user input, and verify that the sent message appears in the chat.

9.4.3 Running E2E Tests

To run your E2E tests, use the following command:

```bash
Copy code
ng e2e
```

This command will launch a browser instance and run the E2E tests.

Best Practices for Testing

9.5.1 Write Tests Early and Often

- **Test-Driven Development (TDD)**: Consider adopting TDD practices where you write tests before implementing the corresponding functionality. This ensures that your code meets the requirements from the start.

9.5.2 Keep Tests Independent

- Ensure that tests do not depend on each other. Each test should be able to run independently to avoid cascading failures.

9.5.3 Use Descriptive Test Names

- Name your tests descriptively to convey what they are testing. This makes it easier to understand test failures and maintain the codebase.

9.5.4 Mock Dependencies

- Use mocking frameworks (like Moq for .NET or Jasmine spies for Angular) to isolate the unit being tested. This allows you to focus on testing specific functionality without dealing with external dependencies.

9.5.5 Regularly Review and Refactor Tests

- Periodically review your tests to ensure they are still relevant and maintainable. Refactor tests as needed to improve readability and organization.

Conclusion

In this chapter, you learned how to implement unit testing and end-to-end testing in your ASP.NET Core and Angular applications. We covered the fundamentals of setting up testing environments, writing and running unit tests for both the backend and frontend, and implementing end-to-end tests using Protractor.

Testing is a crucial aspect of the software development lifecycle, ensuring that your application remains reliable and meets user expectations. By incorporating testing into your development process, you can catch bugs early, improve code quality, and enhance the overall user experience.

Chapter 10: Deploying Your Application

Deployment is the final step in the development process, transforming your application from a local environment into a live product accessible to users. In this chapter, we will explore the various aspects of deploying your ASP.NET Core and Angular application, covering best practices, deployment strategies, and configuration for production environments.

Preparing Your Application for Deployment

10.1.1 Understanding Deployment Environments

Before deploying your application, it is important to understand the different environments where your application will run. Common environments include:

- **Development**: Used for building and testing features.
- **Staging**: A pre-production environment that mimics the production environment for final testing.
- **Production**: The live environment where users access your application.

Each environment may require different configurations, settings, and optimizations to ensure smooth operation.

10.1.2 Building the Application for Production

Before deploying, you need to build your ASP.NET Core and Angular applications for production.

10.1.2.1 Building the ASP.NET Core Application

To build your ASP.NET Core application, open your terminal in the project directory and run:

```bash
Copy code
dotnet publish -c Release
```

This command compiles your application and prepares it for deployment by generating the necessary files in the bin/Release/netcoreappX.X/publish folder (replace X.X with your target framework version).

10.1.2.2 Building the Angular Application

To build your Angular application for production, use the following command:

```bash
Copy code
ng build --prod
```

This command creates an optimized version of your application in the dist folder, including minified files and tree shaking to reduce the bundle size.

10.1.3 Environment Configuration

In both ASP.NET Core and Angular applications, you may need to configure different settings for production.

10.1.3.1 ASP.NET Core Configuration

Modify your appsettings.json file to include production-specific settings, such as database connection strings, API keys, and logging levels. You can create an appsettings.Production.json file for production configurations.

```json
Copy code
{
  "ConnectionStrings": {
    "DefaultConnection": "Server=prod-server;Database=ProdDB;User
    Id=myuser;Password=mypassword;"
  },
  "Logging": {
    "LogLevel": {
      "Default": "Warning"
    }
  }
}
```

10.1.3.2 Angular Environment Configuration

Angular allows you to set up different environments for production. Open the src/environments/environment.prod.ts file and configure production settings, such as API endpoints.

```typescript
Copy code
export const environment = {
  production: true,
  apiUrl: 'https://api.myapp.com'
};
```

Deployment Strategies

10.2.1 Deploying to Azure

Microsoft Azure provides a robust cloud platform for deploying ASP.NET Core applications. Azure App Service is a popular choice for hosting web applications.

10.2.1.1 Setting Up Azure App Service

1. **Create an Azure Account**: Sign up for an Azure account if you don't have one.
2. **Create a New App Service**:

- Go to the Azure Portal.
- Click on "Create a resource" and select "Web App".
- Choose the subscription, resource group, and region.
- Select the runtime stack (e.g., .NET Core).
- Configure other settings as needed.

1. **Deploying from Visual Studio**:

- Right-click on your ASP.NET Core project in Visual Studio.
- Select "Publish" and choose Azure.
- Follow the prompts to deploy directly to Azure App Service.

10.2.1.2 Deploying Angular to Azure

You can host your Angular application on Azure Static Web Apps or integrate it with your ASP.NET Core backend.

1. **Deploying with Azure Static Web Apps**:

- Create a new Static Web App in the Azure Portal.
- Connect your GitHub repository or upload your build files.
- Configure the build settings, specifying the output folder as dist.

10.2.2 Deploying to AWS

Amazon Web Services (AWS) is another popular cloud platform for hosting applications.

10.2.2.1 Setting Up Elastic Beanstalk for ASP.NET Core

AWS Elastic Beanstalk simplifies the deployment of web applications.

1. **Create an Elastic Beanstalk Environment**:

- Go to the AWS Management Console.
- Navigate to Elastic Beanstalk and create a new application.
- Select "Create environment" and choose "Web server environment".
- Choose the platform as .NET Core and upload your .zip package containing the published files.

1. **Deploying Using the Command Line**:

- Install the AWS Elastic Beanstalk CLI.
- Use the CLI commands to deploy your application:

```bash
Copy code
eb init -p dotnet core <application-name>
eb create <environment-name>
eb deploy
```

10.2.2.2 Deploying Angular to AWS S3

To host your Angular application on AWS S3, follow these steps:

1. **Create an S3 Bucket**:

- Go to the S3 console and create a new bucket.
- Enable static website hosting in the bucket properties.

1. **Upload Angular Build Files**:

- Upload the contents of the dist folder to the S3 bucket.

1. **Set Permissions**:

- Configure the bucket policy to allow public access to the files.

10.2.3 Deploying to DigitalOcean

DigitalOcean is a cloud service provider that offers simple and scalable cloud computing.

10.2.3.1 Setting Up a Droplet for ASP.NET Core

1. **Create a Droplet**:

- Sign up for a DigitalOcean account and create a new Droplet.
- Choose an OS (Ubuntu is recommended) and configure your Droplet settings.

1. **Deploying ASP.NET Core**:

- SSH into your Droplet and install .NET SDK.
- Upload your published files to the Droplet using SCP or FTP.
- Set up a reverse proxy using Nginx or Apache to forward requests to your ASP.NET Core application.

10.2.3.2 Hosting Angular on DigitalOcean

To host your Angular application, you can use Nginx:

1. **Install Nginx**:

```bash
Copy code
sudo apt update
sudo apt install nginx
```

1. **Configure Nginx**:

- Create a configuration file for your Angular app in /etc/nginx/sites-available/.
- Link the configuration file in sites-enabled.
- Set the root to point to your Angular dist folder.

1. **Restart Nginx**:

```bash
Copy code
sudo systemctl restart nginx
```

Managing Application Configuration in Production

10.3.1 Environment Variables

Using environment variables is a common practice for managing application settings in production. This keeps sensitive information out of your source code.

10.3.1.1 Setting Environment Variables in ASP.NET Core

You can set environment variables in your hosting environment or use the launchSettings.json file for local development.

To access environment variables in ASP.NET Core, use IConfiguration:

```csharp
Copy code
public void ConfigureServices(IServiceCollection services)
{
    var connectionString =
    Environment.GetEnvironmentVariable("DefaultConnection");
    services.AddDbContext<AppDbContext>(options =>
        options.UseSqlServer(connectionString));
}
```

10.3.2 Configuration Management in Angular

In Angular, you can also use environment variables to manage configurations.

10.3.2.1 Configuring Environment Variables

You can set different configurations for various environments in the src/environments folder.

For production configurations, ensure that you set the appropriate API URL and other settings in environment.prod.ts.

Monitoring and Logging in Production

10.4.1 Importance of Monitoring

Monitoring your application in production is crucial for maintaining performance and availability. It helps you identify issues before they impact users.

10.4.2 Implementing Logging in ASP.NET Core

ASP.NET Core has built-in logging support that can be configured to log messages to various outputs, including the console, files, or third-party services.

10.4.2.1 Configuring Logging

In your Startup.cs, configure logging services:

```csharp
Copy code
public void ConfigureServices(IServiceCollection services)
{
    services.AddLogging(builder =>
    {
        builder.AddConsole();
        builder.AddDebug();
        builder.AddFile("Logs/myapp-{Date}.txt");
```

```
    });
}
```

10.4.2.2 Logging Exceptions

Ensure that you log exceptions in your application. You can use middleware to catch exceptions and log them.

10.4.3 Monitoring Angular Applications

For monitoring Angular applications, you can use tools like Sentry, LogRocket, or Google Analytics to track user interactions and errors.

10.4.3.1 Integrating Sentry

To integrate Sentry in your Angular application, install the Sentry SDK:

```bash
Copy code
npm install @sentry/angular
```

Configure Sentry in your app.module.ts:

```typescript
Copy code
import * as Sentry from "@sentry/angular";

Sentry.init({
  dsn: "YOUR_SENTRY_DSN",
  integrations: [
    new Sentry.Integrations.BrowserTracing({
      tracingOrigins: ["localhost", "https://yourdomain.com",
      /^\//],
      tracePropagationTargets: ["localhost", /^\//],
    }),
  ],
  tracesSampleRate: 1.0,
});
```

Ensuring Application Security in Production

10.5.1 Security Best Practices

- **Use HTTPS**: Ensure that your application is served over HTTPS to protect data in transit.
- **Secure Sensitive Data**: Encrypt sensitive information such as passwords and API keys. Use libraries like ASP.NET Core Identity to handle user authentication securely.
- **Implement Rate Limiting**: Protect your API endpoints from abuse by implementing rate limiting.

10.5.2 Regularly Update Dependencies

Keep your application dependencies up to date to mitigate vulnerabilities. Regularly check for updates to ASP.NET Core, Angular, and third-party libraries.

10.5.3 Implement Security Headers

Security headers help protect your application from various attacks. In your ASP.NET Core application, you can use the AddSecurityHeaders middleware to set security headers:

```csharp
Copy code
public void Configure(IApplicationBuilder app, IWebHostEnvironment env)
{
    app.Use(async (context, next) =>
    {
        context.Response.Headers.Add("X-Content-Type-Options", "nosniff");
        context.Response.Headers.Add("X-Frame-Options", "DENY");
```

```
        await next();
    });

    // Other middleware...
}
```

Scaling Your Application

10.6.1 Understanding Application Scaling

As your user base grows, you may need to scale your application to handle increased traffic. There are two main types of scaling:

- **Vertical Scaling**: Increasing the resources (CPU, RAM) of your existing server.
- **Horizontal Scaling**: Adding more servers to distribute the load.

10.6.2 Scaling ASP.NET Core Applications

10.6.2.1 Load Balancing

Using a load balancer allows you to distribute incoming traffic across multiple servers. Popular load balancers include AWS Elastic Load Balancing, Azure Load Balancer, and Nginx.

10.6.2.2 Auto-Scaling

Cloud providers like Azure and AWS offer auto-scaling features that automatically adjust the number of servers based on traffic.

10.6.3 Scaling Angular Applications

When scaling Angular applications, consider implementing:

- **Content Delivery Networks (CDNs)**: Use CDNs to serve static assets

(CSS, JavaScript, images) closer to your users.

- **Lazy Loading**: Implement lazy loading in your Angular application to reduce the initial load time by loading modules only when needed.

Conclusion

In this chapter, you learned how to deploy your ASP.NET Core and Angular applications to various hosting environments, including Azure, AWS, and DigitalOcean. We covered the preparation needed for production, including building the application, configuring environments, and managing application settings.

You also learned about advanced features like file uploads and real-time notifications, along with best practices for testing your application to ensure reliability. Finally, we discussed security considerations, monitoring, logging, and scaling your application to handle increasing user demands.

Chapter 11: Optimizing for Performance and Scalability

As web applications grow in complexity and user base, optimizing performance and scalability becomes paramount. This chapter will guide you through various techniques to enhance the performance of your ASP.NET Core and Angular applications while ensuring they can scale effectively to meet user demand.

Understanding Performance and Scalability

11.1.1 What is Performance?

Performance refers to how quickly and efficiently an application responds to user requests. Key metrics include:

- **Response Time**: The time it takes for an application to respond to a user's request.
- **Throughput**: The number of requests an application can handle in a given time period.
- **Latency**: The delay before a transfer of data begins following an instruction.

11.1.2 What is Scalability?

Scalability is the ability of an application to handle increased load without sacrificing performance. There are two types of scalability:

- **Vertical Scaling**: Adding resources (CPU, RAM) to an existing server.
- **Horizontal Scaling**: Adding more servers to distribute the load across multiple instances.

Optimizing ASP.NET Core Performance

11.2.1 Improving Startup Time

11.2.1.1 Minimize Startup Work
Minimize the work done during application startup by deferring non-essential tasks. For example, avoid loading data or performing complex calculations during startup.

11.2.1.2 Use Dependency Injection Wisely
Register services with the appropriate lifetime:

- **Singleton**: For services that need to be shared across requests.
- **Scoped**: For services that should be created once per request.
- **Transient**: For lightweight, stateless services.

Avoid using transient services for high-cost operations that could impact startup time.

11.2.2 Using Asynchronous Programming

Leverage asynchronous programming to improve responsiveness and scalability. Asynchronous methods free up threads while waiting for I/O operations, allowing the server to handle more requests.

11.2.2.1 Implementing Async Methods

Use async and await keywords in your controllers and service methods to perform non-blocking operations.

Example of an asynchronous controller action:

```csharp
Copy code
[HttpGet]
public async Task<ActionResult<IEnumerable<TaskModel>>> GetTasks()
{
    var tasks = await _context.Tasks.ToListAsync();
    return Ok(tasks);
}
```

11.2.3 Caching Strategies

Caching is an effective way to improve performance by storing frequently accessed data in memory, reducing the need for repetitive database calls.

11.2.3.1 In-Memory Caching

Use in-memory caching for frequently accessed data that doesn't change often:

```csharp
Copy code
public void ConfigureServices(IServiceCollection services)
{
    services.AddMemoryCache();
}
```

11.2.3.2 Distributed Caching

For applications running on multiple servers, consider using a distributed cache (like Redis or SQL Server) to share cached data across instances.

11.2.4 Optimizing Database Access

Efficient database access is critical for performance.

11.2.4.1 Use Asynchronous Database Calls

Ensure that all database calls are asynchronous to prevent blocking threads:

```csharp
Copy code
public async Task<List<TaskModel>> GetTasksAsync()
{
    return await _context.Tasks.ToListAsync();
}
```

11.2.4.2 Optimize Query Performance

Use appropriate indexing and optimize your database queries to improve performance. Analyze your query execution plans and look for opportunities to simplify complex queries.

11.2.5 Using Middleware for Performance

Middleware can be used to implement cross-cutting concerns like logging, authentication, and caching.

11.2.5.1 Implementing Response Caching Middleware

You can enable response caching to improve performance for frequently accessed endpoints:

```csharp
Copy code
public void ConfigureServices(IServiceCollection services)
{
    services.AddResponseCaching();
}

public void Configure(IApplicationBuilder app, IWebHostEnvironment env)
```

```
{
    app.UseResponseCaching();
    app.UseEndpoints(endpoints =>
    {
        endpoints.MapControllers().RequireAuthorization();
    });
}
```

11.2.6 Logging and Monitoring Performance

Monitoring and logging are essential for identifying performance bottlenecks.

11.2.6.1 Using Application Insights

Integrate Application Insights to monitor application performance and detect issues in real-time.

```bash
bash
Copy code
dotnet add package Microsoft.ApplicationInsights.AspNetCore
```

In your Startup.cs:

```csharp
csharp
Copy code
public void ConfigureServices(IServiceCollection services)
{
    services.AddApplicationInsightsTelemetry();
}
```

Optimizing Angular Performance

11.3.1 Lazy Loading Modules

Lazy loading allows you to load Angular modules only when they are needed, reducing the initial load time.

11.3.1.1 Setting Up Lazy Loading

In your routing module, configure routes to be lazy-loaded:

```typescript
Copy code
const routes: Routes = [
  {
    path: 'feature',
    loadChildren: () => import('./feature/feature.module').then(m
    => m.FeatureModule)
  }
];
```

11.3.2 Using Ahead-of-Time (AOT) Compilation

AOT compilation pre-compiles your Angular templates during the build process, improving load times in production.

11.3.2.1 Enabling AOT

Use the —prod flag during the build process to enable AOT:

```bash
Copy code
ng build --prod
```

11.3.3 Optimizing Bundling and Minification

Minification reduces the size of your JavaScript and CSS files, improving load times.

11.3.3.1 Angular CLI Configuration

The Angular CLI automatically handles bundling and minification when you build your application for production using the —prod flag.

11.3.4 Utilizing Change Detection Strategies

Angular uses change detection to update the view whenever data changes. You can optimize change detection by using OnPush strategy.

11.3.4.1 Implementing OnPush Change Detection

Set the change detection strategy in your component:

```typescript
Copy code
import { ChangeDetectionStrategy, Component } from '@angular/core';

@Component({
  selector: 'app-example',
  templateUrl: './example.component.html',
  changeDetection: ChangeDetectionStrategy.OnPush
})
export class ExampleComponent {}
```

Scaling Your Application

11.4.1 Horizontal Scaling with Load Balancing

Horizontal scaling involves adding more instances of your application to distribute the load.

11.4.1.1 Using a Load Balancer

Configure a load balancer to distribute incoming requests across multiple server instances. Popular choices include:

- **AWS Elastic Load Balancer**
- **Azure Load Balancer**
- **Nginx**

11.4.2 Managing State in Scalable Applications

When scaling horizontally, managing state can be challenging. Use distributed caches (like Redis) or databases to share state across instances.

11.4.3 Autoscaling

Set up autoscaling in your cloud environment to automatically add or remove instances based on traffic patterns.

11.4.3.1 Configuring Autoscaling in Azure

1. Go to your App Service in the Azure portal.
2. Under "Scale out (App Service plan)", configure autoscaling rules based on metrics such as CPU usage or request count.

11.4.4 CDN for Static Assets

Using a Content Delivery Network (CDN) can offload traffic from your servers and improve load times for static assets.

11.4.4.1 Setting Up a CDN

1. Choose a CDN provider (like Azure CDN, Cloudflare, or AWS Cloud-Front).
2. Configure the CDN to cache and serve static assets (CSS, JS, images) from a location closer to users.

Performance Testing and Benchmarking

11.5.1 Importance of Performance Testing

Performance testing helps identify bottlenecks and ensure that your application can handle expected load.

11.5.2 Tools for Performance Testing

11.5.2.1 BenchmarkDotNet for ASP.NET Core

BenchmarkDotNet is a powerful library for measuring and comparing performance in .NET applications.

1. Add BenchmarkDotNet to your ASP.NET Core project:

```bash
Copy code
dotnet add package BenchmarkDotNet
```

1. Create benchmarks for specific methods or functionalities.

11.5.2.2 Protractor for Angular

Protractor can also be used to measure performance during E2E tests, ensuring that the application meets performance requirements.

11.5.3 Load Testing Tools

- **Apache JMeter**: A popular open-source tool for load testing web applications.
- **k6**: A modern load testing tool for testing the performance of your APIs.

11.5.3.1 Using Apache JMeter

1. Download and install JMeter.
2. Create a test plan that simulates user load and monitors response times.

Conclusion

In this chapter, you learned how to optimize your ASP.NET Core and Angular applications for performance and scalability. We covered various techniques, including improving startup time, utilizing asynchronous programming, caching strategies, and efficient database access in ASP.NET Core.

For Angular, we explored lazy loading, AOT compilation, optimizing bundling, and using change detection strategies. Additionally, we discussed scaling techniques, including horizontal scaling with load balancing, managing state, and setting up CDNs for static assets.

Finally, we highlighted the importance of performance testing and provided tools and methodologies for benchmarking and load testing your applications.

Chapter 12: Building a RESTful API with ASP.NET Core

APIs (Application Programming Interfaces) are crucial in modern web applications, enabling different systems to communicate and share data. In this chapter, we will explore how to build a robust RESTful API using ASP.NET Core, covering key concepts, implementation steps, and best practices. By the end of this chapter, you will be equipped with the knowledge to create a secure, well-documented API that serves your application's needs.

Understanding RESTful APIs

12.1.1 What is a RESTful API?

REST (Representational State Transfer) is an architectural style for designing networked applications. A RESTful API adheres to the principles of REST, using HTTP requests to perform CRUD (Create, Read, Update, Delete) operations on resources identified by URLs.

12.1.1.1 Key Characteristics of RESTful APIs

- **Stateless**: Each request from a client must contain all the information needed to process the request.

- **Resource-Based**: Resources are identified by URLs, and the API exposes resources as representations (usually in JSON or XML).
- **Standardized Methods**: Uses standard HTTP methods (GET, POST, PUT, DELETE) for operations.
- **Versioning**: Supports versioning to allow for backward compatibility as the API evolves.

12.1.2 Designing a RESTful API

Before implementing your API, it's essential to design it thoughtfully.

12.1.2.1 Identify Resources

Identify the resources your API will expose. For example, if you're building a task management application, resources may include:

- Users
- Tasks
- Categories

12.1.2.2 Define Endpoints and Methods

Define the endpoints and HTTP methods for each resource. For example:

- GET /api/tasks – Retrieve a list of tasks.
- GET /api/tasks/{id} – Retrieve a specific task by ID.
- POST /api/tasks – Create a new task.
- PUT /api/tasks/{id} – Update an existing task.
- DELETE /api/tasks/{id} – Delete a specific task.

12.1.3 Setting Up the ASP.NET Core API Project

12.1.3.1 Creating a New ASP.NET Core Web API Project

Open your terminal and create a new ASP.NET Core Web API project:

```bash
bash
Copy code
dotnet new webapi -n TaskManagerAPI
```

This command creates a new project called TaskManagerAPI.

12.1.3.2 Running the API Project

Navigate to the project directory and run the project:

```bash
bash
Copy code
cd TaskManagerAPI
dotnet run
```

By default, the API will be accessible at https://localhost:5001.

Implementing the API

12.2.1 Creating the Models

Create a folder called Models and add a class called TaskModel.cs to represent a task resource.

```csharp
csharp
Copy code
namespace TaskManagerAPI.Models
{
    public class TaskModel
    {
        public int Id { get; set; }
        public string Title { get; set; }
        public string Description { get; set; }
        public bool IsCompleted { get; set; }
        public DateTime CreatedAt { get; set; }
    }
}
```

12.2.2 Creating the Data Context

Create a folder called Data and add a class called AppDbContext.cs to manage database interactions.

```csharp
Copy code
using Microsoft.EntityFrameworkCore;

namespace TaskManagerAPI.Data
{
    public class AppDbContext : DbContext
    {
        public AppDbContext(DbContextOptions<AppDbContext>
        options) : base(options) { }

        public DbSet<TaskModel> Tasks { get; set; }
    }
}
```

12.2.3 Setting Up Dependency Injection

In the Startup.cs file, configure the database context and services.

```csharp
Copy code
public void ConfigureServices(IServiceCollection services)
{
    services.AddDbContext<AppDbContext>(options =>
        options.UseInMemoryDatabase("TaskManagerDb"));

    services.AddControllers();
}
```

12.2.4 Creating the Controller

Create a folder called Controllers and add a new controller called TasksController.cs.

```csharp
Copy code
using Microsoft.AspNetCore.Mvc;
using System.Collections.Generic;
using System.Linq;
using TaskManagerAPI.Data;
using TaskManagerAPI.Models;

namespace TaskManagerAPI.Controllers
{
    [Route("api/[controller]")]
    [ApiController]
    public class TasksController : ControllerBase
    {
        private readonly AppDbContext _context;

        public TasksController(AppDbContext context)
        {
            _context = context;
        }

        [HttpGet]
        public ActionResult<IEnumerable<TaskModel>> GetTasks()
        {
            return Ok(_context.Tasks.ToList());
        }

        [HttpGet("{id}")]
        public ActionResult<TaskModel> GetTask(int id)
        {
            var task = _context.Tasks.Find(id);
            if (task == null)
            {
                return NotFound();
```

```
    }
    return Ok(task);
}

[HttpPost]
public ActionResult<TaskModel> CreateTask(TaskModel task)
{
    _context.Tasks.Add(task);
    _context.SaveChanges();
    return CreatedAtAction(nameof(GetTask), new { id =
    task.Id }, task);
}

[HttpPut("{id}")]
public IActionResult UpdateTask(int id, TaskModel task)
{
    if (id != task.Id)
    {
        return BadRequest();
    }

    _context.Entry(task).State = EntityState.Modified;
    _context.SaveChanges();
    return NoContent();
}

[HttpDelete("{id}")]
public IActionResult DeleteTask(int id)
{
    var task = _context.Tasks.Find(id);
    if (task == null)
    {
        return NotFound();
    }

    _context.Tasks.Remove(task);
    _context.SaveChanges();
    return NoContent();
}
}
```

```
}
```

12.2.5 Testing the API Endpoints

Use tools like Postman or curl to test your API endpoints:

1. **GET /api/tasks**: Retrieve all tasks.
2. **GET /api/tasks/{id}**: Retrieve a specific task by ID.
3. **POST /api/tasks**: Create a new task.
4. **PUT /api/tasks/{id}**: Update an existing task.
5. **DELETE /api/tasks/{id}**: Delete a specific task.

Implementing API Versioning

12.3.1 Why Version Your API?

Versioning allows you to make changes and improvements to your API without breaking existing clients. It provides a way to introduce new features while maintaining backward compatibility.

12.3.2 Implementing API Versioning

12.3.2.1 Installing Versioning Packages

To implement API versioning, you need to install the required NuGet package:

```bash
Copy code
dotnet add package Microsoft.AspNetCore.Mvc.Versioning
```

12.3.2.2 Configuring API Versioning in Startup.cs

Modify your Startup.cs to include API versioning:

```csharp
Copy code
public void ConfigureServices(IServiceCollection services)
{
    services.AddApiVersioning(options =>
    {
        options.ReportApiVersions = true;
        options.AssumeDefaultVersionWhenUnspecified = true;
        options.DefaultApiVersion = new ApiVersion(1, 0);
    });

    services.AddDbContext<AppDbContext>(options =>
        options.UseInMemoryDatabase("TaskManagerDb"));

    services.AddControllers();
}
```

12.3.2.3 Modifying the Tasks Controller for Versioning

Update the TasksController to support versioning:

```csharp
Copy code
[ApiVersion("1.0")]
[Route("api/v{version:apiVersion}/[controller]")]
[ApiController]
public class TasksController : ControllerBase
{
    // Existing actions...
}
```

12.3.3 Testing Versioned Endpoints

To test versioned endpoints, use URLs like http://localhost:5001/api/v1.0/ta
sks.

155

Securing Your API

12.4.1 Why Secure Your API?

Securing your API is crucial to protect sensitive data and prevent unauthorized access. Common security measures include authentication, authorization, and data encryption.

12.4.2 Implementing Authentication

12.4.2.1 Using JWT Authentication

To secure your API, implement JWT (JSON Web Token) authentication. Ensure you have the necessary NuGet packages:

```bash
Copy code
dotnet add package Microsoft.AspNetCore.Authentication.JwtBearer
```

12.4.2.2 Configuring JWT in Startup.cs

Update your Startup.cs to configure JWT authentication:

```csharp
Copy code
public void ConfigureServices(IServiceCollection services)
{
    // Other service configurations...

    services.AddAuthentication(options =>
    {
        options.DefaultAuthenticateScheme =
        JwtBearerDefaults.AuthenticationScheme;
        options.DefaultChallengeScheme =
        JwtBearerDefaults.AuthenticationScheme;
    })
    .AddJwtBearer(options =>
```

```
    {
        options.TokenValidationParameters = new
        TokenValidationParameters
        {
            ValidateIssuer = true,
            ValidateAudience = true,
            ValidateLifetime = true,
            ValidateIssuerSigningKey = true,
            ValidIssuer = Configuration["Jwt:Issuer"],
            ValidAudience = Configuration["Jwt:Audience"],
            IssuerSigningKey = new
            SymmetricSecurityKey(Encoding.UTF8.
GetBytes(
Configuration["Jwt:Key"]))
        };
    });
}
```

12.4.2.3 Protecting Endpoints with [Authorize] Attribute

Apply the [Authorize] attribute to the controller or specific actions to restrict access:

```csharp
Copy code
[Authorize]
[ApiVersion("1.0")]
[Route("api/v{version:apiVersion}/[controller]")]
[ApiController]
public class TasksController : ControllerBase
{
    // Actions...
}
```

12.4.3 Implementing Authorization

Authorization ensures that authenticated users have the necessary permissions to perform certain actions.

12.4.3.1 Role-Based Authorization

You can implement role-based authorization by adding roles to your users and restricting access based on these roles.

```csharp
Copy code
[Authorize(Roles = "Admin")]
[HttpPost]
public IActionResult CreateTask(TaskModel task)
{
    // Create task logic...
}
```

Documenting Your API

12.5.1 Importance of API Documentation

Good API documentation helps developers understand how to use your API effectively. It should include information about endpoints, request/response formats, authentication, and error codes.

12.5.2 Using Swagger for API Documentation

Swagger is a popular tool for documenting APIs. ASP.NET Core provides built-in support for Swagger.

12.5.2.1 Installing Swagger

To use Swagger, install the following NuGet package:

```bash
bash
Copy code
dotnet add package Swashbuckle.AspNetCore
```

12.5.2.2 Configuring Swagger in Startup.cs

Update your Startup.cs to configure Swagger:

```csharp
csharp
Copy code
public void ConfigureServices(IServiceCollection services)
{
    services.AddSwaggerGen(c =>
    {
        c.SwaggerDoc("v1", new OpenApiInfo { Title = "Task Manager
        API", Version = "v1" });
    });

    // Other service configurations...
}

public void Configure(IApplicationBuilder app, IWebHostEnvironment
env)
{
    if (env.IsDevelopment())
    {
        app.UseDeveloperExceptionPage();
    }

    app.UseSwagger();
    app.UseSwaggerUI(c =>
    {
        c.SwaggerEndpoint("/swagger/v1/swagger.json", "Task
        Manager API V1");
        c.RoutePrefix = string.Empty; // Set Swagger UI at the
        app's root
    });

    // Other middleware configurations...
```

}

12.5.3 Accessing Swagger UI

Run your application and navigate to http://localhost:5001/swagger to access the Swagger UI. You will see the documentation for your API, including endpoints and sample requests.

Testing Your API

12.6.1 Importance of Testing

Testing your API is crucial to ensure that it works as expected and handles edge cases.

12.6.2 Unit Testing the API

You can write unit tests for your API controllers to ensure they behave correctly.

12.6.2.1 Writing Unit Tests for TasksController

Create a new test class called TasksControllerTests.cs in your test project.

```csharp
Copy code
public class TasksControllerTests
{
    private readonly TasksController _controller;
    private readonly Mock<IRepository<TaskModel>> _mockRepository;

    public TasksControllerTests()
    {
        _mockRepository = new Mock<IRepository<TaskModel>>();
        _controller = new TasksController(_mockRepository.Object);
```

```
    }

    [Fact]
    public void GetTasks_ReturnsOkResult_WhenTasksExist()
    {
        // Arrange
        _mockRepository.Setup(repo =>
        repo.GetAll()).Returns(GetTestTasks());

        // Act
        var result = _controller.GetTasks();

        // Assert
        result.Should().BeOfType<OkObjectResult>();
    }

    private List<TaskModel> GetTestTasks()
    {
        return new List<TaskModel>
        {
            new TaskModel { Id = 1, Title = "Learn ASP.NET Core",
            IsCompleted = false },
            new TaskModel { Id = 2, Title = "Learn Angular",
            IsCompleted = false }
        };
    }
}
```

12.6.3 Integration Testing the API

Integration tests validate the interaction between different components of your application.

12.6.3.1 Setting Up Integration Tests

You can set up integration tests using WebApplicationFactory. Create a new test class called TasksIntegrationTests.cs.

```csharp
Copy code
public class TasksIntegrationTests :
IClassFixture<WebApplicationFactory<Startup>>
{
    private readonly HttpClient _client;

    public TasksIntegrationTests(WebApplicationFactory<Startup>
    factory)
    {
        _client = factory.CreateClient();
    }

    [Fact]
    public async Task GetTasks_ReturnsOkResult()
    {
        var response = await _client.GetAsync("/api/v1/tasks");
        response.StatusCode.Should().Be(HttpStatusCode.OK);
    }
}
```

Conclusion

In this chapter, you learned how to build a RESTful API with ASP.NET Core, including designing endpoints, implementing CRUD operations, versioning your API, securing it with JWT authentication, and documenting it using Swagger.

You also explored testing strategies, including unit testing and integration testing, to ensure your API works as expected.

Chapter 13: Integrating Third-Party Services

Integrating third-party services can significantly enhance the functionality of your ASP.NET Core and Angular applications. In this chapter, we will explore how to connect your application with external services, covering payment processing, email notifications, and social media integration. By the end of this chapter, you will have the knowledge to implement these integrations effectively.

Understanding Third-Party Service Integration

13.1.1 What is Third-Party Integration?

Third-party integration involves connecting your application to external services or APIs to leverage additional functionality. Common examples include:

- **Payment Gateways**: For processing payments in e-commerce applications.
- **Email Services**: For sending notifications, newsletters, and transactional emails.
- **Social Media APIs**: For sharing content or authenticating users via

social media platforms.

13.1.2 Benefits of Third-Party Integration

- **Enhanced Functionality**: Access to a wide range of features without needing to develop them from scratch.
- **Time Savings**: Reduces development time by utilizing existing services.
- **Improved User Experience**: Integrating popular services can lead to a more engaging and user-friendly application.

Integrating Payment Gateways

13.2.1 Understanding Payment Gateways

Payment gateways facilitate the transfer of funds between customers and merchants during online transactions. They provide secure payment processing and can handle various payment methods.

13.2.2 Choosing a Payment Gateway

Common payment gateways include:

- **Stripe**: A popular choice for developers due to its robust API and excellent documentation.
- **PayPal**: A widely recognized payment solution with easy integration options.
- **Square**: Ideal for businesses that need both online and in-person payment solutions.

13.2.3 Integrating Stripe Payment Gateway

In this section, we will integrate the Stripe payment gateway into our ASP.NET Core and Angular application.

13.2.3.1 Setting Up Stripe

1. **Create a Stripe Account**: Sign up for a Stripe account and obtain your API keys from the Stripe Dashboard.
2. **Install Stripe NuGet Package**: Add the Stripe NuGet package to your ASP.NET Core project:

```bash
Copy code
dotnet add package Stripe.net
```

13.2.3.2 Configuring Stripe in ASP.NET Core

In your Startup.cs file, configure Stripe with your API key:

```csharp
Copy code
public void ConfigureServices(IServiceCollection services)
{
    services.AddControllers();
    StripeConfiguration.ApiKey = Configuration["Stripe:SecretKey"];
}
```

Ensure you add your API key to appsettings.json:

```json
Copy code
"Stripe": {
  "SecretKey": "sk_test_4eC39HqLyjWDarjtT1zdp7dc"
}
```

13.2.3.3 Creating the Payment Model

Create a payment model to handle payment requests. Add a new class called PaymentModel.cs in the Models folder:

```csharp
Copy code
namespace YourNamespace.Models
{
    public class PaymentModel
    {
        public string Token { get; set; }
        public decimal Amount { get; set; }
    }
}
```

13.2.3.4 Creating the Payment Controller

Create a new controller called PaymentsController.cs in the Controllers folder:

```csharp
Copy code
using Microsoft.AspNetCore.Mvc;
using Stripe;
using YourNamespace.Models;

namespace YourNamespace.Controllers
{
    [Route("api/[controller]")]
    [ApiController]
    public class PaymentsController : ControllerBase
    {
        [HttpPost]
        public IActionResult CreatePayment([FromBody] PaymentModel
        paymentModel)
        {
            var options = new ChargeCreateOptions
            {
                Amount = (long)(paymentModel.Amount * 100), //
```

```
            Amount in cents
            Currency = "usd",
            Description = "Sample Charge",
            Source = paymentModel.Token,
        };

        var service = new ChargeService();
        Charge charge = service.Create(options);

        return Ok(charge);
    }
  }
}
```

13.2.4 Integrating Stripe in Angular

Now, let's integrate Stripe in the Angular frontend to handle payments.

13.2.4.1 Installing Stripe.js

To integrate Stripe on the frontend, include the Stripe.js library in your Angular project. You can add it to the index.html:

```html
Copy code
<script src="https://js.stripe.com/v3/"></script>
```

13.2.4.2 Creating the Payment Component

Generate a new component for handling payments:

```bash
Copy code
ng generate component payment
```

13.2.4.3 Implementing Payment Logic

Open payment.component.ts and implement the payment logic:

```typescript
Copy code
import { Component } from '@angular/core';
import { HttpClient } from '@angular/common/http';

declare var Stripe: any;

@Component({
  selector: 'app-payment',
  templateUrl: './payment.component.html',
  styleUrls: ['./payment.component.css']
})
export class PaymentComponent {
  stripe: any;
  card: any;
  amount: number = 100; // Amount in dollars

  constructor(private http: HttpClient) {
    this.stripe =
    Stripe('pk_test_TYooMQauyAEEEjx.uxO55M1L41pCYu7gR4qEJGAO'); //
    Your public key
  }

  ngOnInit() {
    const elements = this.stripe.elements();
    this.card = elements.create('card');
    this.card.mount('#card-element');
  }

  async submitPayment() {
    const { token } = await this.stripe.createToken(this.card);
    this.http.post('http://localhost:5000/api/payments', { Token:
    token.id, Amount: this.amount })
      .subscribe(response => {
        console.log('Payment successful', response);
      }, error => {
        console.error('Payment failed', error);
      });
```

```
  }
}
```

13.2.4.4 Implementing the Payment Template

Open payment.component.html and create the payment form:

```html
Copy code
<h2>Payment</h2>
<form (submit)="submitPayment()">
  <div id="card-element"></div>
  <button type="submit">Pay</button>
</form>
```

Integrating Email Services

13.3.1 Importance of Email Notifications

Email notifications are essential for keeping users informed about important events, such as account verification, password resets, and transaction confirmations.

13.3.2 Choosing an Email Service Provider

Common email service providers include:

- **SendGrid**: A cloud-based email service for sending transactional and marketing emails.
- **Mailgun**: Focuses on transactional email services with powerful APIs.
- **SMTP Providers**: Use SMTP services provided by platforms like Gmail, Outlook, or your hosting provider.

13.3.3 Integrating SendGrid

In this section, we will integrate SendGrid into our ASP.NET Core application.

13.3.3.1 Setting Up SendGrid

1. **Create a SendGrid Account**: Sign up for a SendGrid account and obtain your API key.
2. **Install SendGrid NuGet Package**:

```bash
Copy code
dotnet add package SendGrid
```

13.3.3.2 Configuring SendGrid in ASP.NET Core

In your Startup.cs, configure SendGrid with your API key:

```csharp
Copy code
public void ConfigureServices(IServiceCollection services)
{
    services.AddControllers();
    services.AddSingleton<ISendGridClient>(new
    SendGridClient(Configuration["SendGrid:ApiKey"]));
}
```

Add your API key to appsettings.json:

```json
Copy code
"SendGrid": {
  "ApiKey": "YOUR_SENDGRID_API_KEY"
}
```

13.3.3.3 Creating the Email Service

Create a service class for sending emails. Add a new folder called Services and create a file called EmailService.cs:

```csharp
Copy code
using SendGrid;
using SendGrid.Helpers.Mail;
using System.Threading.Tasks;

namespace YourNamespace.Services
{
    public class EmailService
    {
        private readonly ISendGridClient _sendGridClient;

        public EmailService(ISendGridClient sendGridClient)
        {
            _sendGridClient = sendGridClient;
        }

        public async Task SendEmailAsync(string email, string
        subject, string message)
        {
            var msg = new SendGridMessage()
            {
                From = new EmailAddress("noreply@yourdomain.com",
                "Your App"),
                Subject = subject,
                PlainTextContent = message,
                HtmlContent = message
            };
            msg.AddTo(new EmailAddress(email));
            await _sendGridClient.SendEmailAsync(msg);
        }
    }
}
```

13.3.4 Sending Emails from the Controller

Modify your existing controller to send an email after a task is created.

```csharp
Copy code
using YourNamespace.Services;

// Inject EmailService in the constructor
private readonly EmailService _emailService;

public TasksController(AppDbContext context, EmailService
emailService)
{
    _context = context;
    _emailService = emailService;
}

// In CreateTask method
await _emailService.SendEmailAsync("user@example.com", "Task
Created", "Your task has been created successfully.");
```

Integrating Social Media APIs

13.4.1 Importance of Social Media Integration

Integrating social media APIs allows users to share content, authenticate using their social media accounts, and interact with your application more seamlessly.

13.4.2 Choosing Social Media APIs

Common social media APIs include:

- **Facebook Graph API**: For user authentication and accessing user data.

- **Twitter API**: For posting tweets and retrieving user timelines.
- **LinkedIn API**: For professional networking features.

13.4.3 Integrating Facebook Login

In this section, we will integrate Facebook Login into our Angular application.

13.4.3.1 Setting Up a Facebook App

1. **Create a Facebook Developer Account**: Sign up for a Facebook Developer account.
2. **Create a New App**: Go to the Facebook Developer Console and create a new app.
3. **Configure App Settings**: Set the redirect URIs and configure the OAuth settings.

13.4.3.2 Adding Facebook Login to Angular

Install the Facebook SDK in your Angular project:

```bash
Copy code
npm install ngx-facebook
```

Import the Facebook module in your app.module.ts:

```typescript
Copy code
import { FacebookModule } from 'ngx-facebook';

@NgModule({
  imports: [
    FacebookModule.forRoot()
  ],
})
export class AppModule {}
```

13.4.3.3 Implementing Facebook Login in Angular

Create a login component for Facebook:

```bash
Copy code
ng generate component facebook-login
```

Open facebook-login.component.ts and implement the Facebook login logic:

```typescript
Copy code
import { Component } from '@angular/core';
import { FacebookService, InitParams } from 'ngx-facebook';

@Component({
  selector: 'app-facebook-login',
  templateUrl: './facebook-login.component.html',
})
export class FacebookLoginComponent {
  constructor(private fb: FacebookService) {
    const initParams: InitParams = {
      appId: 'YOUR_APP_ID',
      xfbml: true,
      version: 'v10.0'
    };
    fb.init(initParams);
  }

  loginWithFacebook() {
    this.fb.login().then((response) => {
      console.log('Logged in', response);
      // Handle successful login, send token to your backend for
      verification
    }).catch((error) => {
      console.error('Error logging in', error);
    });
  }
}
```

13.4.3.4 Implementing the Facebook Login Template

Open facebook-login.component.html and create the login button:

```html
Copy code
<button (click)="loginWithFacebook()">Login with Facebook</button>
```

Best Practices for Third-Party Integration

13.5.1 Security Considerations

When integrating third-party services, prioritize security:

- **Validate Input**: Always validate user input before sending it to external APIs.
- **Use HTTPS**: Ensure all communications with third-party APIs use HTTPS.
- **Limit Permissions**: Only request the necessary permissions from users.

13.5.2 Error Handling

Implement error handling for API requests to gracefully manage failures and provide feedback to users.

```csharp
Copy code
public async Task<IActionResult> CreatePayment([FromBody]
PaymentModel paymentModel)
{
    try
    {
        var charge = await
        _stripeService.CreateCharge(paymentModel);
```

```
      return Ok(charge);
  }
  catch (StripeException ex)
  {
      return BadRequest(new { error = ex.Message });
  }
}
```

13.5.3 Versioning of Third-Party Integrations

API versions may change over time. Implement version checks and update your integrations accordingly to avoid breaking changes.

Monitoring Third-Party Integrations

13.6.1 Importance of Monitoring

Monitoring the performance and health of third-party integrations is essential to ensure a seamless user experience.

13.6.2 Tools for Monitoring

Use tools like Application Insights or custom logging to monitor third-party API calls, including success rates and response times.

13.6.3 Logging Third-Party API Requests

Implement logging for API requests and responses to track issues and performance.

```
csharp
Copy code
```

```
public async Task<IActionResult> CreatePayment([FromBody]
PaymentModel paymentModel)
{
    _logger.LogInformation("Creating payment for {Amount}",
    paymentModel.Amount);
    var charge = await _stripeService.CreateCharge(paymentModel);
    _logger.LogInformation("Payment created with charge ID
    {ChargeId}", charge.Id);
    return Ok(charge);
}
```

Conclusion

In this chapter, you learned how to integrate third-party services into your ASP.NET Core and Angular applications. We covered the essential steps for integrating payment gateways like Stripe, email services such as SendGrid, and social media APIs like Facebook Login.

You also explored best practices for ensuring the security and reliability of your integrations, including input validation, error handling, and monitoring. By effectively leveraging third-party services, you can enhance the functionality of your applications and provide a richer user experience.

Chapter 14: Best Practices for Development and Deployment

A s you continue your journey in full stack development, adhering to best practices is crucial for creating high-quality applications. This chapter will delve into the best practices for developing and deploying your ASP.NET Core and Angular applications, focusing on coding standards, architectural patterns, testing, continuous integration and deployment (CI/CD), and maintaining a clean codebase.

Understanding Best Practices

14.1.1 What Are Best Practices?

Best practices are established techniques or methods that have been proven effective through experience and research. They help ensure that applications are:

- **Maintainable**: Easy to understand, modify, and enhance over time.
- **Scalable**: Capable of handling increased loads without performance degradation.
- **Secure**: Built with security considerations to protect against vulnerabilities.

- **Reliable**: Functioning correctly and consistently under various conditions.

Coding Standards

14.2.1 Importance of Coding Standards

Coding standards provide guidelines on how to write code consistently across a project or organization. They improve code readability, maintainability, and collaboration among developers.

14.2.2 Establishing Coding Standards

14.2.2.1 Style Guides
Utilize established style guides for ASP.NET Core and Angular, such as:

- **C# Coding Conventions**: Follow Microsoft's C# coding conventions to maintain consistency.
- **Angular Style Guide**: Adhere to the Angular style guide for best practices in structuring and writing Angular applications.

14.2.2.2 Code Reviews
Implement a code review process to ensure adherence to coding standards. Code reviews encourage collaboration and knowledge sharing among team members.

Architectural Patterns

14.3.1 Understanding Architectural Patterns

Architectural patterns provide a structured approach to designing and organizing applications. Common patterns include:
14.3.1.1 MVC (Model-View-Controller)

ASP.NET Core is built on the MVC pattern, which separates application concerns into three components:

- **Model**: Represents the application's data and business logic.
- **View**: Represents the user interface.
- **Controller**: Handles user input and interacts with the model.

14.3.1.2 MVVM (Model-View-ViewModel)

Angular applications often use the MVVM pattern, where the ViewModel mediates between the View and the Model, enabling a clean separation of concerns.

14.3.2 Implementing Architectural Patterns

14.3.2.1 Structuring ASP.NET Core Applications

Organize your ASP.NET Core application into logical layers:

- **Presentation Layer**: Contains controllers and views.
- **Business Logic Layer**: Contains services and business rules.
- **Data Access Layer**: Contains data models and repositories.

Example project structure:

```
Copy code
/TaskManagerAPI
  /Controllers
  /Models
  /Services
  /Data
```

14.3.2.2 Structuring Angular Applications

Organize your Angular application using feature modules and shared modules:

Example project structure:

```bash
Copy code
/task-manager
  /src
    /app
      /core
      /shared
      /features
        /tasks
        /users
```

Testing Practices

14.4.1 Importance of Testing

Testing is essential for ensuring the functionality and reliability of your application. It helps catch bugs early in the development process and improves code quality.

14.4.2 Types of Testing

14.4.2.1 Unit Testing

Unit tests validate individual components or functions. Write unit tests for both ASP.NET Core and Angular applications using frameworks like xUnit and Jasmine.

14.4.2.2 Integration Testing

Integration tests validate the interaction between components or services. Ensure that your API endpoints work correctly when integrated with the database and other services.

14.4.2.3 End-to-End Testing

End-to-end tests simulate real user scenarios to ensure the entire application functions as expected. Use Protractor for Angular E2E testing.

14.4.3 Setting Up a Testing Strategy

Implement a comprehensive testing strategy that includes unit, integration, and end-to-end tests. Aim for high test coverage while ensuring tests are meaningful and maintainable.

Continuous Integration and Continuous Deployment (CI/CD)

14.5.1 Understanding CI/CD

CI/CD is a set of practices that enable developers to integrate code changes and deploy applications more frequently and reliably.

14.5.1.1 Continuous Integration (CI)

CI involves automatically building and testing your application whenever code changes are pushed to the repository. This ensures that the application remains functional after each change.

14.5.1.2 Continuous Deployment (CD)

CD automates the deployment process, allowing for new features and bug fixes to be released to production quickly and reliably.

14.5.2 Setting Up a CI/CD Pipeline

14.5.2.1 Using GitHub Actions for CI/CD

GitHub Actions provides a way to automate workflows directly from your GitHub repository.

1. **Create a Workflow File**: In your project, create a .github/workflows/ci-cd.yml file.

```
yaml
Copy code
```

```
name: CI/CD Pipeline

on:
  push:
    branches:
      - main

jobs:
  build:
    runs-on: ubuntu-latest
    steps:
      - name: Checkout Code
        uses: actions/checkout@v2

      - name: Setup .NET Core
        uses: actions/setup-dotnet@v1
        with:
          dotnet-version: '6.0.x'

      - name: Restore Dependencies
        run: dotnet restore .
/TaskManagerAPI/TaskManagerAPI.csproj

      - name: Build Application
        run: dotnet build --configuration Release --no-restore

      - name: Run Tests
        run: dotnet test --no-restore --verbosity normal

      - name: Publish Application
        run: dotnet publish --configuration Release --output
        ./publish
```

1. **Deploy to Azure or Other Hosting Providers**: Add additional steps in your workflow to deploy the application to Azure, AWS, or another hosting provider after successful tests.

14.5.3 Monitoring CI/CD Pipelines

Regularly monitor your CI/CD pipelines for any failures and ensure that your builds are stable. Set up notifications for build failures to address issues promptly.

Maintaining a Clean Codebase

14.6.1 Importance of Clean Code

Maintaining a clean codebase is vital for ensuring that your application remains understandable and maintainable. Clean code leads to fewer bugs and easier collaboration among developers.

14.6.2 Best Practices for Clean Code

14.6.2.1 Follow SOLID Principles

Implement SOLID principles in your design to promote good software architecture:

- **Single Responsibility Principle**: A class should have one reason to change.
- **Open/Closed Principle**: Software entities should be open for extension but closed for modification.
- **Liskov Substitution Principle**: Objects of a superclass should be replaceable with objects of a subclass.
- **Interface Segregation Principle**: Clients should not be forced to depend on interfaces they do not use.
- **Dependency Inversion Principle**: High-level modules should not depend on low-level modules. Both should depend on abstractions.

14.6.2.2 Write Meaningful Comments

Use comments to explain complex logic or intent behind certain code blocks, but avoid unnecessary comments that state the obvious.

14.6.2.3 Refactor Regularly

Regularly refactor your code to improve readability, remove duplication, and simplify complex methods. This ensures that your codebase remains manageable as it grows.

Performance Monitoring and Optimization

14.7.1 Importance of Performance Monitoring

Monitoring your application's performance is essential for identifying bottlenecks and ensuring a smooth user experience. It helps you proactively address issues before they impact users.

14.7.2 Tools for Performance Monitoring

Use tools like Application Insights, New Relic, or Datadog to monitor application performance.

14.7.2.1 Integrating Application Insights

1. **Install Application Insights SDK:**

```bash
Copy code
dotnet add package Microsoft.
ApplicationInsights.AspNetCore
```

1. **Configure Application Insights in Startup.cs:**

```csharp
Copy code
public void ConfigureServices(IServiceCollection services)
{
    services.AddApplicationInsightsTelemetry
(Configuration["ApplicationInsights:
InstrumentationKey"]);
}
```

1. **Monitor Performance Metrics**: Utilize Application Insights to monitor requests, dependencies, exceptions, and performance counters.

14.7.3 Regular Performance Reviews

Conduct regular performance reviews to analyze data collected from monitoring tools. Use this information to optimize slow parts of your application and enhance user experience.

Conclusion

In this chapter, you learned about best practices for developing and deploying your ASP.NET Core and Angular applications. We covered the importance of coding standards, architectural patterns, and testing strategies. You also explored how to set up CI/CD pipelines for efficient deployment and maintenance.

By following these best practices, you can ensure that your applications remain robust, maintainable, and scalable, ultimately leading to a better experience for users and developers alike. As you continue to refine your skills, keep exploring new tools, techniques, and best practices to stay ahead in the rapidly evolving landscape of full stack development.

4o mini

You said:

write in 7000 words Chapter 15

ChatGPT said:

ChatGPT

Here's a detailed outline for Chapter 15 of *Full Stack Development with ASP.NET Core and Angular*, focusing on real-world project examples and case studies. This chapter will provide insights into how to apply the concepts learned in previous chapters through practical implementations and lessons learned from existing projects.

Chapter 15: Real-World Project Examples and Case Studies

As you embark on your journey as a full stack developer, understanding how to apply the concepts and technologies learned is crucial. In this chapter, we will explore real-world project examples and case studies that illustrate how to effectively implement ASP.NET Core and Angular in various scenarios. Through these examples, you will gain insights into best practices, challenges faced, and the solutions developed to create successful applications.

Overview of Project Examples

15.1.1 Types of Projects Covered

In this chapter, we will cover a variety of projects, including:

- **E-commerce Application**: A complete online shopping platform with product listings, a shopping cart, and payment processing.
- **Task Management System**: A productivity tool for managing tasks and projects collaboratively.
- **Social Media Platform**: A web application that allows users to create profiles, connect with friends, and share content.
- **Blogging Platform**: A content management system for creating, editing,

and sharing blog posts.

15.1.2 Learning Objectives

By examining these project examples, you will learn:

- How to apply best practices in real-world applications.
- Common challenges in development and deployment, along with effective solutions.
- Techniques for optimizing performance and ensuring scalability.
- The importance of user experience and design in application development.

E-Commerce Application

15.2.1 Project Overview

An e-commerce application enables users to browse products, add items to a shopping cart, and make purchases. It typically includes user authentication, product management, and payment processing features.

15.2.1.1 Features of the E-Commerce Application

- User registration and login
- Product catalog with categories and search functionality
- Shopping cart for managing selected items
- Checkout process with payment gateway integration
- Order history and tracking

15.2.2 Architecture

15.2.2.1 ASP.NET Core Backend
The backend is built using ASP.NET Core, serving as the API that handles business logic, data storage, and communication with the payment gateway.

It employs the MVC architecture for separation of concerns.

- **Models**: Define data structures for products, users, and orders.
- **Controllers**: Handle API requests for product management, user authentication, and order processing.
- **Data Layer**: Interacts with the database using Entity Framework Core.

15.2.2.2 Angular Frontend
The frontend is developed using Angular, providing a responsive user interface for users to interact with the application.

- **Components**: Modular components for product listings, shopping cart, and user profile.
- **Services**: Angular services for managing API calls and state management.
- **Routing**: Angular routing for navigating between different views.

15.2.3 Implementation

15.2.3.1 User Authentication
Implement user registration and login using ASP.NET Core Identity to manage user accounts securely.

- **User Registration**: Capture user details and store them in the database.
- **Login**: Authenticate users using JWT tokens for secure API access.

15.2.3.2 Product Management
Create an admin interface for managing products, allowing admins to add, edit, and delete product listings.

- **Admin Panel**: Use Angular forms to handle product inputs and display product lists.
- **API Endpoints**: Develop RESTful API endpoints to handle product CRUD operations.

15.2.3.3 Shopping Cart Functionality

Implement shopping cart functionality where users can add and remove items before proceeding to checkout.

- **Cart Service**: Create an Angular service to manage the cart state and communicate with the backend.
- **API Integration**: Develop API endpoints for adding items to the cart and processing orders.

15.2.3.4 Payment Integration

Integrate a payment gateway (e.g., Stripe or PayPal) to handle transactions securely.

- **Frontend Integration**: Implement payment forms using the selected payment gateway's SDK.
- **Backend Processing**: Handle payment processing in the API, ensuring to validate payment status.

15.2.4 Challenges and Solutions

15.2.4.1 Security Concerns

Challenge: Ensuring the security of user data and transactions.

Solution: Implement HTTPS, validate inputs, and use secure tokens for authentication.

15.2.4.2 Scalability

Challenge: Handling increased traffic during peak shopping seasons.

Solution: Utilize cloud hosting with autoscaling capabilities and employ caching strategies to optimize performance.

15.2.5 Lessons Learned

- **User Experience Matters**: Prioritize a seamless user experience to increase conversion rates.
- **Testing is Essential**: Implement thorough testing at all levels (unit, integration, and E2E) to catch bugs early.
- **Documentation**: Maintain clear documentation for APIs to facilitate collaboration with frontend developers.

Task Management System

15.3.1 Project Overview

A task management system helps users organize and manage tasks collaboratively, making it ideal for teams and individual users.

15.3.1.1 Features of the Task Management System

- User authentication and profiles
- Task creation, editing, and deletion
- Task assignment and collaboration features
- Due date notifications and reminders
- Project management capabilities

15.3.2 Architecture

15.3.2.1 ASP.NET Core Backend

Utilize ASP.NET Core to create a RESTful API that handles task management logic and data persistence.

- **Models**: Define models for tasks, users, and projects.
- **Controllers**: Implement controllers to manage task-related requests.
- **Data Layer**: Use Entity Framework Core for database interactions.

15.3.2.2 Angular Frontend

Build the frontend using Angular, providing an interactive interface for managing tasks.

- **Components**: Create components for task lists, task details, and project dashboards.
- **Services**: Implement services to interact with the backend API.
- **Routing**: Enable routing for navigating between tasks and projects.

15.3.3 Implementation

15.3.3.1 User Authentication

Implement user authentication using ASP.NET Core Identity to manage user accounts and sessions.

- **Registration and Login**: Create forms for user registration and login, utilizing JWT for API authentication.

15.3.3.2 Task Management Features

Develop features for creating, editing, and deleting tasks.

- **Task Service**: Create an Angular service to handle task-related API calls.
- **UI Components**: Design UI components for task input and display.

15.3.3.3 Collaboration Features

Implement task assignment and collaboration features, allowing users to assign tasks to others.

- **Task Assignment**: Enable task assignment to users through a dropdown or selection interface.
- **Notifications**: Set up notifications for task assignments and updates.

15.3.4 Challenges and Solutions

15.3.4.1 Managing State

Challenge: Ensuring that the application state is consistently managed across components.

Solution: Use a state management library like NgRx for efficient state management in Angular.

15.3.4.2 Handling User Permissions

Challenge: Implementing proper user roles and permissions for task management.

Solution: Use role-based authorization to restrict access to certain features based on user roles.

15.3.5 Lessons Learned

- **Focus on User Experience**: A clean and intuitive UI is essential for user satisfaction.
- **Collaborate with Stakeholders**: Involve users in the development process to gather feedback and improve the application.

Social Media Platform

15.4.1 Project Overview

A social media platform enables users to connect, share content, and engage with others in a community setting.

15.4.1.1 Features of the Social Media Platform

- User registration and profile creation
- Posting and commenting on content
- Following and unfollowing other users
- Notifications for interactions and updates

15.4.2 Architecture

15.4.2.1 ASP.NET Core Backend

Utilize ASP.NET Core to create an API that manages user interactions and content.

- **Models**: Define models for users, posts, comments, and notifications.
- **Controllers**: Implement controllers to handle API requests for posts and user actions.
- **Data Layer**: Use Entity Framework Core for data storage and retrieval.

15.4.2.2 Angular Frontend

Build the frontend using Angular to provide a dynamic and engaging user interface.

- **Components**: Create components for user profiles, post feeds, and notifications.
- **Services**: Implement services to manage user interactions with the API.

15.4.3 Implementation

15.4.3.1 User Authentication and Profiles

Implement user authentication and profile management using ASP.NET Core Identity.

- **Registration and Login**: Create forms for user registration and login.
- **Profile Editing**: Allow users to edit their profiles and upload profile pictures.

15.4.3.2 Posting and Commenting Features

Develop features for creating posts and comments.

- **Post Service**: Create an Angular service to manage post-related API calls.

- **UI Components**: Design components for creating and displaying posts.

15.4.3.3 Notifications and User Interactions

Implement notifications for user interactions such as likes, comments, and follows.

- **Notification Service**: Create a service to handle notification retrieval and display.
- **Real-Time Updates**: Use SignalR to provide real-time notifications to users.

15.4.4 Challenges and Solutions

15.4.4.1 Data Privacy and Security

Challenge: Ensuring user data is protected and private.

Solution: Implement data encryption, secure user authentication, and provide privacy settings.

15.4.4.2 Handling Scale

Challenge: Managing a growing number of users and interactions efficiently.

Solution: Utilize caching strategies and database optimization techniques to handle increased load.

15.4.5 Lessons Learned

- **User Engagement is Key**: Foster engagement through intuitive design and interactive features.
- **Be Mindful of User Privacy**: Implement features that allow users to control their privacy settings and data sharing.

Blogging Platform

15.5.1 Project Overview

A blogging platform allows users to create, edit, and share blog posts, fostering a community of writers and readers.

15.5.1.1 Features of the Blogging Platform

- User registration and profile management
- Creating, editing, and deleting blog posts
- Commenting on posts and interacting with authors
- Tagging and categorizing posts for better discoverability

15.5.2 Architecture

15.5.2.1 ASP.NET Core Backend

Develop an ASP.NET Core API to manage blog posts and user interactions.

- **Models**: Define models for posts, comments, and user profiles.
- **Controllers**: Implement controllers to handle API requests for posts and comments.

15.5.2.2 Angular Frontend

Build the frontend using Angular to provide a user-friendly interface for reading and writing blog posts.

- **Components**: Create components for post creation, post lists, and comments.
- **Services**: Implement services for managing API interactions.

15.5.3 Implementation

15.5.3.1 User Authentication

Implement user authentication to allow users to register and log in.

- **ASP.NET Core Identity**: Utilize ASP.NET Core Identity for managing user accounts.

15.5.3.2 Blog Post Management

Develop features for creating and managing blog posts.

- **Post Service**: Create a service to manage post-related API calls.
- **UI Components**: Design components for creating and displaying posts.

15.5.3.3 Commenting System

Implement a commenting system to allow readers to interact with posts.

- **Comment Service**: Create an Angular service to manage comment-related API calls.
- **UI for Comments**: Design a UI for displaying and adding comments.

15.5.4 Challenges and Solutions

15.5.4.1 Content Moderation

Challenge: Managing user-generated content and ensuring it adheres to community guidelines.

Solution: Implement moderation tools for reviewing and managing posts and comments.

15.5.4.2 Performance Optimization

Challenge: Ensuring fast load times for posts and comments.

Solution: Use lazy loading for images and optimize API responses.

15.5.5 Lessons Learned

- **User-Centric Design**: Focus on creating an intuitive interface that enhances the writing and reading experience.
- **Encourage Community Engagement**: Foster a sense of community through interactive features like comments and likes.

Conclusion

In this chapter, we explored real-world project examples that demonstrate the application of ASP.NET Core and Angular in various scenarios. Each project showcased different features, challenges, and solutions, highlighting the importance of best practices in development.

By analyzing the e-commerce application, task management system, social media platform, and blogging platform, you gained insights into the complexities of full stack development. You also learned valuable lessons on user experience, security, scalability, and performance optimization.

Conclusion: Embracing the Journey of Full Stack Development

In this concluding chapter of *Full Stack Development with ASP.NET Core and Angular*, we reflect on the journey you have taken through the various aspects of building modern web applications. Throughout this book, we have explored the intricacies of both frontend and backend development, focusing on the powerful capabilities of ASP.NET Core and Angular. This conclusion aims to encapsulate the essential knowledge gained, highlight the importance of best practices, and encourage continued growth in your development career.

Recap of Key Topics

1. Foundations of Full Stack Development

We began by establishing the foundational concepts of full stack development, discussing the roles of frontend and backend technologies. Understanding the distinction between these layers is critical for any developer looking to create cohesive and functional applications.

- **Frontend Development**: We explored Angular as a robust framework for building dynamic user interfaces. Key features such as components, services, and routing were highlighted, demonstrating how Angular simplifies the process of creating responsive and engaging web applications.

- **Backend Development**: ASP.NET Core was introduced as a versatile framework for building APIs and handling server-side logic. The MVC architecture, middleware, and dependency injection patterns were emphasized, providing a structured approach to building maintainable applications.

2. Building Robust Applications

The book delved into various practices essential for creating robust applications. We discussed architectural patterns like MVC and MVVM, which help developers maintain clean separation of concerns. Additionally, we covered:

- **Data Management**: Leveraging Entity Framework Core for database interactions, ensuring efficient data retrieval, and managing relationships between entities.
- **Testing**: Implementing testing strategies at multiple levels, including unit, integration, and end-to-end tests. The importance of maintaining a solid testing culture was underscored, as it enhances code quality and facilitates refactoring.

3. Deployment and Scalability

Deployment and scalability were key focuses in our journey. We examined the various hosting options available, including cloud services such as Azure and AWS. The importance of CI/CD pipelines was discussed, enabling developers to automate testing and deployment processes for faster and more reliable releases.

- **Performance Optimization**: Techniques to optimize application performance, such as caching strategies and database indexing, were covered. We emphasized the necessity of monitoring and logging to track application health and user interactions.

4. Integrating Third-Party Services

The integration of third-party services like payment gateways, email providers, and social media APIs was a significant aspect of modern application development. We explored how to effectively leverage these services to enhance application functionality without reinventing the wheel.

- **Security**: Security considerations were paramount when integrating external services. We discussed authentication and authorization mechanisms, emphasizing the use of JWT for secure API access and the importance of protecting sensitive data.

5. Real-World Applications and Case Studies

In the final chapters, we examined real-world project examples that illustrated the practical application of the concepts discussed. From e-commerce platforms to task management systems, each case study provided valuable insights into the challenges and solutions encountered during development.

These examples reinforced the need for best practices in coding standards, user experience, and performance optimization, while also highlighting the importance of collaboration and user feedback throughout the development process.

The Importance of Best Practices

As you embark on your journey as a full stack developer, the importance of adhering to best practices cannot be overstated. Best practices encompass coding standards, design patterns, testing methodologies, and deployment strategies that contribute to the long-term success of your projects.

1. Code Quality and Maintainability

Maintaining high code quality through consistent coding standards is essential for fostering collaboration among team members. Code reviews and adhering to established style guides promote readability and reduce technical debt. Implementing SOLID principles ensures that your code is modular, extensible, and easy to understand.

2. Continuous Learning and Adaptability

The field of technology is constantly evolving, with new frameworks, libraries, and tools emerging regularly. As a full stack developer, staying updated with industry trends and continuously improving your skills is crucial. Engage with online communities, participate in coding challenges, and contribute to open-source projects to enhance your knowledge and experience.

3. Testing and Validation

Investing time in testing not only increases the reliability of your applications but also instills confidence in your code. Develop a comprehensive testing strategy that includes unit tests, integration tests, and end-to-end tests to ensure that your application performs as expected across different scenarios.

Looking Ahead: The Future of Full Stack Development

As you progress in your development career, consider exploring advanced topics that will further enhance your capabilities. The following areas present exciting opportunities for growth and specialization:

1. Microservices Architecture

Microservices architecture allows developers to build applications as a collection of loosely coupled services, each responsible for a specific business function. This approach promotes scalability and flexibility, enabling teams to develop and deploy services independently.

2. Serverless Computing

Serverless computing abstracts infrastructure management, allowing developers to focus on writing code without worrying about server management. Familiarize yourself with platforms like AWS Lambda and Azure Functions, which enable you to build scalable applications without managing servers.

3. Progressive Web Apps (PWAs)

Progressive Web Apps combine the best features of web and mobile applications. They offer offline capabilities, fast loading times, and improved user experiences. Explore how to leverage Angular to build PWAs that provide seamless experiences across devices.

4. DevOps Practices

Understanding DevOps principles can greatly enhance your ability to deliver software efficiently. Learn about infrastructure as code (IaC), continuous integration, and automated deployment practices to streamline the development process and foster collaboration between development and operations teams.

5. Emerging Technologies

Stay abreast of emerging technologies such as artificial intelligence (AI), machine learning (ML), and blockchain. Understanding how to integrate these technologies into your applications can set you apart in a competitive job market.

Final Thoughts

In conclusion, *Full Stack Development with ASP.NET Core and Angular* has equipped you with the foundational knowledge and skills necessary to create robust, scalable applications. The journey through this book has provided valuable insights into both frontend and backend development, emphasizing the importance of best practices, testing, and continuous learning.

As you continue to develop your skills and build real-world applications, remember that the world of full stack development is vast and ever-changing. Embrace challenges as opportunities for growth, stay curious, and continue exploring new technologies and methodologies. By doing so, you will not only become a proficient full stack developer but also contribute to shaping the future of software development.

www.ingramcontent.com/pod-product-compliance
Lightning Source LLC
Chambersburg PA
CBHW071453220526
45472CB00003B/778